ECONOMICS, ECOLOGY, AND THE ROOTS OF WESTERN FAITH

ECONOMICS, ECOLOGY, AND THE ROOTS OF WESTERN FAITH

Perspectives from the Garden

Robert R. Gottfried

ROWMAN & LITTLEFIELD PUBLISHERS, INC.

ROWMAN & LITTLEFIELD PUBLISHERS, INC.

Published in the United States of America
by Rowman & Littlefield Publishers, Inc.
4720 Boston Way, Lanham, Maryland 20706

3 Henrietta Street
London WC2E 8LU, England

British Cataloging in Publication Information Available

Library of Congress Cataloging-in-Publication Data
Gottfried, Robert R.
Economics, ecology, and the roots of Western faith : perspectives
from the garden / by Robert R. Gottfried.
p. cm.
Includes bibliographical references and index.
1. Human ecology–Religious aspects–Christianity. 2. Economics–
Religious aspects–Christianity. I. Title.
BT695.5.G68 1995 261.8'362–dc20 95-14492 CIP

0-8476-8016-9 (cloth: alk. paper)
0-8476-8017-7 (pbk.: alk. paper)

Printed in the United States of America

∞ TM The paper used in this publication meets the minimum requirements of
American National Standard for Information Sciences—Permanence of
Paper for Printed Library Materials, ANSI Z39.48–1984.

Contents

Preface

This book started, as many projects do, with a conversation. About eleven years ago I was sitting in the snack bar with my friend Patricia Killen, then a professor of the School of Theology of the University of the South (Sewanee). We often met to share a cup of coffee. That day I expressed to her my interest in the relationship between humans and the environment and in biblical insights on the matter. She responded, "Robin, maybe you're supposed to write a book on environmental theology." These words, spoken by a theologian to an economist, boggled my mind.

A lot has happened since then—I have traveled to Puerto Rico and Costa Rica to work on questions of environment and development, collaborated with ecologists on research projects, taught and discussed ideas with students and colleagues, and written this book. Although this is not a work of environmental theology, Patricia's words turned out to be prophetic.

I have grown a great deal in researching and writing this book. It represents my best thinking on these issues at the moment. However, in a work of such breadth inevitably something will be left out or misconstrued—particularly in fields not my own. For these errors of omission and commission, I ask your forgiveness. Feel free to share your thoughts with me.

I have benefited from the expertise and encouragement of many people, particularly John Cobb, emeritus professor at Claremont School of Theology, and Walter Brueggemann of Columbia Seminary, who have encouraged me and guided me along the way. I owe a great deal to them and to the following, who also critiqued drafts of various chapters and encouraged me to keep going: Douglas Booth of the Department of Economics at Marquette University; Robert Bradford, publications editor at Sewanee; Charles Brockett of the Political Science Department at Sewanee; Jim Dunkly, head librarian of Sewanee's School of Theology library; Jill Hendrickson of Sewanee's Economics Department; Guy Lytle, Dean of Sewanee's School of Theology; Yasmeen Mohiuddin of Sewanee's Economics Department; Philip Powell, graduate student in economics at Vanderbilt University; George Ramseur, emeritus professor of biology at Sewanee; Sarah Warren, formerly of the Department of Natural Resources at Sewanee; Clyde Tilley, former professor of religion at Union University; and Rebecca Wright of Sewanee's School of Theology. My special thanks go to ecologist Yolande Gottfried, my ever-patient and loving wife. Without them, their enthusiasm, and their expertise, this book would have remained a wonderful idea. Thanks also to Dean Freudenberger of Luther Northwestern Theological Seminary who early on encouraged me to explore these issues. While all these people have greatly improved this study, I fully accept responsibility for any shortcomings it still might have.

In the process of working with them on our joint projects, I have learned a great deal from Richard Flamm, Robert Lee, Robert Naiman, Robert Twilley, Monica Turner, and David Wear. In many ways, they, too, are part of this work.

I wish to thank the University of the South for providing me with release time to read and write. Without that support this book might never have materialized.

Many thanks, also, to the editorial staff at Rowman & Littlefield, particularly Jon Sisk, Jennifer Ruark, and Julie Kirsch, whose faith in this work, and able and efficient editing, helped give it birth. I appreciate their efforts greatly.

Finally, and most fundamentally, I stand in awe of and gratitude to the Song who flows through, and in, all creation, bringing insight and life. Only because of your inspiration and insistence does this book exist. I dedicate my work to you and to my family, great mediators of your love and care. Thank you.

Chapter 1

Introduction

Today many Westerners seem to yearn for a return to the Garden, a place where humans and the natural world relate intimately to one another. Pilgrimages to India, Native American vision quests, New Age religion, Deep Ecology philosophy, and numerous other movements attract increasing numbers of people who sense that they lack rootedness in the earth. Christianity, the long-dominant religion of the West, seems irrelevant and distant from a world where people relate intimately to the natural world. Indeed, many join Lynn White (1967) in viewing Christianity as the main culprit for our rootlessness and for the environmental degradation increasingly evident around us. White stated that the injunction in the Bible's book of Genesis to "subdue the earth" lies at the root of Western humanity's relentless exploitation of nature. According to White and many others, the West does whatever it wants with the earth because its people believe that the earth was given to them for that purpose.

At the same time, many environmentalists blame modern economics for much environmental degradation. They claim that this human-centered, profit-oriented, individualistic discipline ignores both ecological reality and the intrinsic worth of other organisms. In many ways, economics reflects the view that nature doesn't matter.

To a degree, the critics of both Christianity and modern economics may be right. As Tucker (1993) says with respect to the injunction to "subdue the earth,"

Lift that injunction out of context, take it individualistically instead of corporately, combine it with a Calvinistic work ethic, throw in the industrial revolution, and the result is indeed an ecological crisis. How one understands human destiny, and especially the place of human beings in

1

and with the world, certainly has made a difference, and certainly will continue to do so. (p. 108)

Western Christianity and economics have adopted Western culture, including all the biases stemming from the Enlightenment, which elevated reason to the status of a god and objectified nature. Whether Christianity as it existed at that time fostered this approach, or adopted it, lies outside the focus of the following pages. However, it is clear that adherents of popular Christianity and of Western culture, including many economists, believe that humans have been given the earth to do with as they please, and that their behavior with respect to nature has no consequences. Westerners seem to believe that their spiritual and physical well-being depends little upon nature, aside from the effects of water and air pollution.

The story I wish to tell differs radically. We have no need to look to cultures that, rich and valuable as they are, lie outside our own traditions. If we dig back far enough, to the beginning of the Common Era (the time of Christ), we find a civilization whose writing left us a rich legacy of thought and spirituality replete with economic, political, and ecological implications.[1] The Hebrews of that period and the early Christians who emerged from that Jewish culture possessed a set of attitudes and beliefs with respect to nature that differ greatly from popular beliefs today. In fact, the Hebrew Bible, or Old Testament, provides "perhaps the most important single source of Western popular images, if not concepts, of creation" (Clifford 1988, p. 151). This compendium of writings spanning many centuries provides a rich archive ready to be mined by people seeking ways to relate to nature that fit modern circumstances.

Similarly, a study of ecology reveals many principles that fit well with the Hebrew perspective and that offer economics the potential for a far more adequate understanding of the interrelationships between ecological vitality and human well-being. Ecology's holistic perspective and attention to spatial relationships offer economics exciting insights into the ecological foundations for economic activity.

While Western Christianity and economics may have lost their ecological consciousness along the way, this does not imply that they cannot recoup it. By examining our cultural roots, we can discover a body of thought remarkably modern in its orientation and well suited to dealing with problems of environmental degradation, human welfare, and injustice. In a similar fashion we gain much from an understanding of some basic ecological concepts and how they may affect our understanding of the world.

This does not mean that one must become Jewish or Christian to become environmentally sensitive in a Western way. One can learn from these religions without joining them. Those who count themselves within these faiths may find their faith strengthened and enriched by what follows. Similarly, we don't all have to become ecologists to become environmentally literate. Rather, we all stand to regain our connection to the earth by returning to our cultural roots and understanding this faith's coherence with modern science.

The Importance of Relationship

For people interested in humanity's relationship with its natural environment, the faith of the Hebrew people offers great insight. These people believed that the Holy One of Israel creates and sustains all things. This "creation faith" served as the fundamental theme with which the Jewish people interpreted their history and early Christians understood Jesus.[2]

The Jewish people by the time of the Common Era saw things holistically. Individuals did not have separate bodies and spirits that somehow coexisted with, or fought, one another. Rather, mind, spirit, and body all affected one another and comprised one integrated whole. Similarly, people received their individuality through their many relationships with their human and natural surroundings. They lived as members of a society in intimate relationship with their maker and their natural world. As part of one great biophysical-human-spiritual system, they and other humans played a key role in determining its vitality. What they did and believed made a difference. Their attitudes and behaviors brought either prosperity or destruction for all. The entire system depended upon maintaining healthy relationships, understanding how the system functioned, and working with it.

Ecology strikingly resembles this faith in several ways. Once again, relationships reign supreme. On the cellular level, individual cells depend in part upon their complex environment to determine what kind of cell they will become. Certain plants and animals may play key roles in an ecosystem. Removing them may alter the system greatly unless other organisms can replace their functions. If not, the system may change irrevocably. The behaviors of the members of the system have consequences for the entire system. The system also affects each of its components. The entire system depends upon the health of its component parts, just as its parts depend upon the health of the system.

Ecologists also note that, as one moves to larger and larger systems, behaviors become evident that otherwise could not be determined by looking only at smaller scales. Minimal understanding of one scale's processes require at least understanding behaviors at one scale below and above. Examining body organs and summing them up, for instance, does not mean that we understand the human being. Something happens when body organs interact. Similarly, something happens to people when they are placed together in a society. A minimal understanding of humans would require understanding at least how human organs function, how they work together, and how people interact.

Similarly, creation faith tells us that human and natural systems exist within a spiritual matrix where behaviors may emerge that we can understand only by examining the larger-scale system. Understanding human-ecological interrelationships requires that we understand both human and natural processes and the spiritual matrix, while realizing that our human faculties limit our understanding of processes that may occur at the largest scale.

Land Economics and Economic Organization

All of the above imply that economists may have much to learn. Modern neoclassical economics arose out of eighteenth-century British utilitarian philosophy and the revolutionary physics of Isaac Newton. Neoclassical economists view humans as individuals living isolated from one another, their main occupations being production, consumption, and distribution of goods. They receive pleasure or pain from their activities. Modern theory, which attempts at times to apply this approach to families and other social groups, assumes individuals who act ultimately on the basis of their individual gain or loss. The values and preferences that motivate people are given. Neoclassical economics has no theory that explains the creation of these values. Relationships in this framework bear little resemblance to the rich relationships of Jewish or ecological thought.

The natural environment hardly appears in mainline economics except as a source of raw materials and a sink for humanity's waste. Outside of the subfields of environmental and natural resource economics, most modern economic analyses even omit these roles. These subfields of economics do recognize that humans may suffer physically and aesthetically from environmental degradation. However, until recently, environmental and resource economics rarely considered that such degradation might threaten the fundamental existence of an economic system and the basic well-being of its people.

The extent of environmental deterioration today has led growing numbers of economists and ecologists, though still a minority, to attempt to incorporate links between ecological and economic systems to examine the ecological foundations of economic activity and the impacts on them of economic activity. These analyses attempt to forge an understanding of ecosystems and economies as parts of one large system. As such, these efforts support the concerns about ecologically sustainable growth and development, which the Earth Summit of world leaders focused upon in Rio de Janeiro in June 1992.

These analyses raise interesting questions as to the ability of the market and current political institutions to bring about sustainable economic well-being. Can the market or institutions using market forces adequately incorporate ecological systems into the economic system? If not, can governments do so?

Few economists and ecologists have addressed the larger-scale issue presented by Jewish creation faith. Could it be that we still have too narrow a view of humanity and nature? Is it possible that attitudes and beliefs need to change? Do they make a difference? We need to ask what economic development truly entails and what determines sustainability at the largest scale of human activity.

The Image of the Garden

Our modern Western culture leads us to believe that humans live apart from nature, that they are different and separate from it. However, the Jewish tradition at the root of our culture "presents us with a picture of the universe as an ecologically harmonious system of interrelated, interdependent beings. The picture is beautifully expressed in the creational symbol of 'the Garden,' that place of mutuality from which the human being was expelled just because of its bid for autonomy" (Hall 1986, p. 136).

The image of the Garden suggests that our image of autonomy from one another and from nature may be the cause of many of our problems. "Garden" brings to mind primeval paradise, festoons of fruit hanging from trees, gravel paths lined with boxwood, massed flowers arranged geometrically, vegetable patches rich in promise, and seemingly chaotic jumbles of plants surrounding tropical homes. All these gardens mix human intent and ingenuity with natural processes to create systems where plants, animals, and humans may interact and flourish. They reveal rich patterns of human and natural mutuality.

Using the image of the Garden offers several advantages. First, ecologically we can view gardens as managed natural systems. What we plant, where we plant, what we plant together with other plants, and when we plant, all determine the structure of the system. Some gardens include forests as an integral part of their design. How much we clear and whether or not we weed, mulch, or apply pesticides also determine what plants and animals will live there and what types of relationships will exist therein. Thus, the Garden reminds us that ecological relationships matter when we deal with nature. Second, the Garden also brings to consciousness the feeling that we somehow lost a primeval paradise and wish to regain it. It conjures up faint memories of long-lost relationships that drive us to seek reconciliation with nature and some greater spirit. Third, gardens are particular places with particular appearances. The Garden reminds us that economics plays itself out on landscapes, that economics deals with places that have their own unique characteristics. Economists typically avoid spatial relationships and characteristics. Finally, the expulsion from the Garden reminds us that our behavior has grave consequences. We stand accountable for what we do.

The Economics of the Garden

For these reasons I choose to talk about the economics of the Garden. In doing so I bring together insights from ecology, the creation faith of the Bible, and economics to examine humanity's relationship with nature. Discussing these questions inevitably leads me to deal with values.

The value assumptions economists make critically affect everything they do. Values affect the questions economists ask, the analytical conclusions they draw, and the policy prescriptions they offer (Schumacher 1973, chap. 4; Kneese and Sweeney 1985; Pearce and Turner 1990, chap. 15; Toman 1994). When examining sustainability (the ability of an economy to maintain human well-being over many generations), neoclassical economists have encountered many difficulties in extending individual concepts of fairness to equity between generations. Toman (1994) concludes that an "organicist" (holistic or stewardship) approach to ethics avoids many of these difficulties. Such an ethic emphasizes safeguarding large-scale ecological processes and stresses that individuals not only seek their own narrowly defined self-interest but also base decisions upon a concern for the larger society. This book outlines such an approach as an alternative to the narrow individualism inherent in neoclassical economics.[3] As might be expected, this holistic approach leads to a different understanding of human welfare and its relationship to the natural world than neoclassical economics offers.

As we shall see, the way we view the world determines the types of options we perceive and the way we behave. As we come to see our world more holistically, we will perceive new opportunities for ways we can relate to each other and to nature. If we are to learn how to live in a Garden, we must rethink our values, lifestyles, relationships, and goals. This book represents a small effort in that direction.

The following pages focus on the relational nature of ecology and creation faith and the way these relationships reveal themselves on the landscape. Chapter 2 develops an ecological understanding of nature, mixing in a bit of economics along the way. It examines the nature of individuality and of ecosystems, raising some important questions such as: Can humans attempt to dominate nature with impunity? Does dominating behavior ultimately strike at the root of what it means to be human? Should we dominate nature, or should we attempt to cooperate with its processes? Can we fully understand the mechanisms that affect our answer, or do we confront problems of scale?

Chapters 3 and 4 explore these issues from a moral perspective by developing the creation faith of the Jewish people at the beginning of the Common Era and its extension into early Christianity. Because that faith failed to distinguish between body and soul, spirit and matter, "creation" embraced the physical, intangible, political, economic, natural, and spiritual in one reality. The Jews recognized that one must understand how the world operates to experience the fullness of life in all of its dimensions.

Accordingly, the remaining chapters address the questions raised in chapter 2 from a social, ecological, and moral perspective. The fifth chapter discusses the interactions between natural systems and the economic system to understand better what sustainable well-being for all of creation might entail. The next to last chapter attempts to examine how "spiritual" malaise wreaks environmental destruction on landscapes. The chapter speculates on how creation faith's insights on environmental degradation may work themselves out concretely on the land. The last chapter then asks how people might best organize to manage their land for themselves and all of creation. Should government or the market take the lead in managing land, or should some other type of institution? Which institutions offer the best hope not only for land management, but also for providing a basis for the sustainable development of society? Based upon the conclusions to these questions, the chapter offers some reflections on the economics of the Garden.

This, then, is our project. Let us begin by examining the nature of nature.

Notes

1. Hall agrees with this assessment. He states, "(T)he religion of the West has been . . . reluctant to admit of any great mystery in the world itself, and has consequently treated the world as if it were a thing—a very large collection of things—put here for human use. The corrective for the situation, however, does not have to be introduced from the East. The 'journey to the East' by numerous sensitive souls in our period might well pause longer than it has wont to do in Jerusalem" (Hall 1986, p. 136).

2. Many Christians today confuse the creation faith of the Jews with science. The Jews concerned themselves with understanding their relationship to the Creator so that they could be faithful to the Creator's intent for their lives. Therefore, they did not worry about the scientific basis for creation—the actual way the Creator creates. After all, science as we know it did not even exist at that time. Accordingly, we cannot expect this prescientific society to be concerned with our scientific questions. The Jewish creation faith dealt with the present world and its natural environment, not so much with its origins (Schmid 1973, pp. 103, 111).

3. Toman also points out that such an approach carries with it the danger that, if the importance of the group vis-à-vis the individual is not constrained, society can assert its supremacy over individual rights and destroy individual liberty. I believe that the view of the world developed in this book provides a strong constraint to the importance of the group. Neoclassical economics carries with it a concomitant, and seldom-recognized danger, that rampant individualism can destroy the consciousness that individuals live in a social context, and can destroy the social context itself. What we need is a view of the world that allows the individual and the group to live in creative tension with one another. I hope that I have succeeded in relating such a vision.

References

Clifford, Richard J. 1988. "Creation in the Hebrew Bible." Pp. 151–70 in *Physics, Philosophy, and Theology: A Common Quest for Understanding*, ed. Robert J. Russell, William R. Stoeger, and G. V. Coyne. Vatican Observatory.

Hall, Douglas John. 1986. *Imaging God: Dominion as Stewardship*. Grand Rapids: W. W. Eerdmans.

Kneese, Allen V., and J. L. Sweeney. 1985. "Ethics and Environmental Economics.'' Pp. 191–220 in *Handbook of Natural Resource and Energy Economics*, ed. Allen V. Kneese, and William D. Schulze. Amsterdam: Elsevier Science Publishers B. V.

Pearce, David W., and R. Kerry Turner. 1990. *Economics of Natural Resources and the Environment*. Baltimore: Johns Hopkins University Press.

Schmid, H. H. 1973. ''Creation, Righteousness, and Salvation: Creation Theology as the Broad Horizon of Biblical Theology.'' Pp. 102–17 in *Creation in the Old Testament*, ed. Bernhard W. Anderson. Philadelphia: Fortress.

Schumacher, E. F. 1973. *Small Is Beautiful: Economics as if People Mattered.* New York: Harper & Row.

Toman, Michael A. 1994. ''Economics and 'Sustainability': Balancing Tradeoffs and Imperatives.'' Discussion paper (January 1991 revised February 1994). Washington, DC: Resources for the Future.

Tucker, Gene M. 1993. ''Creation and the Limits of the World: Nature and History in the Old Testament.'' *Horizons in Biblical Theology* 15 (2): 105–18.

White, Lynn. 1967. ''The Historical Roots of Our Ecologic Crisis.'' *Science* 155 (March 10): 1203–7.

Chapter 2

On Gardens and Gardeners: The Significance of Relationships

In 1870 Ernest Haeckel coined the term "ecology" from the root words *oikos*, "household," and *ology*, "study of." Ecology refers to the study of the household we live in, the plants, animals, atmosphere, soil, and oceans in which and with which we live. He defined it as follows: "By ecology we mean the body of knowledge concerning the economy of nature—the investigation of the total relations of the animal both to its inorganic and to its organic environment; including, above all, its friendly and inimical relations with those animals and plants with which it comes directly or indirectly into contact" (Cobb and Birch 1981, p. 29).

Today we understand ecology as the study of the relationships between and among interdependent beings, and the physical and biological processes that occur among them over time and space. Ecology can be studied at various hierarchical levels: at the individual organism level, at the species or population level (e.g., the behavior of deer herds), and at the community level, where ecologists consider both the plant and animal populations in the same area.

On larger scales, ecologists speak of ecosystems, landscapes, and biomes. When ecologists consider the abiotic (nonliving) environment along with the biotic (living) components, they may refer to this system as an ecosystem. An ecosystem has a boundary, through which inputs and outputs of energy and matter flow. Internal processes influence the rates of flow of the inputs and outputs. Several terrestrial ecosystems (which include humans) may be grouped together to comprise a landscape. Landscapes may be further aggregated in large, regional units known as biomes, such as a tropical rain forest biome, a temperate rain forest biome, or a tundra biome. Continents and oceans form biogeographic regions that have their own unique flora and fauna. Finally, ecologists refer to the collection of all the interacting biogeographic regions as the biosphere. It includes all those portions of the earth where life exists, including the biologically inhabitable soil, air, and water (Odum 1989, pp. 26–28; Woodmansee 1990, pp. 57–71).

The boundaries of these hierarchical systems tend to blend—as among forest types, for example. Drawing the line between one ecosystem and another can be quite arbitrary. On the one hand, ecologists have struggled with the difficulty of delineating boundaries. On the other, when change occurs between two ecosystems, the boundaries—called ecotones—are more easily visible. Stream banks, intertidal zones, and prairie-forest junctions all contain more diverse flora and fauna than the interiors of either ecosystem.

Systems, Individuality, Cooperation, and Human Nature

One of the aspects of ecology that makes it so fascinating is its systems, or holistic, approach. Ecologists feel that one can understand certain levels of behavior of an animal or plant population only by seeing how it interacts with other living organisms and with the abiotic environment. This means that behavior often depends upon the structure of the system, on the relationships between the system's components. At the level of the organism, environmental factors strongly influence behavior. Breeding, for instance, begins when certain stimuli such as day length, temperature, or rainfall reach thresholds that then trigger hormonal changes. Migration similarly begins when certain environmental cues signal that the time is appropriate.[1]

Relationships not only play a large role in determining individual behavior, they also strongly influence the nature of the individual. One can understand both molecular biology and cellular differentiation ecologically. On the genetic level, what a particular DNA molecule does depends upon the particular way molecules in the nonnuclear part of the cell are configured. As cells divide and develop into a multicelled organism, two adjacent cells with identical DNA may develop quite differently—one may become a nerve cell and the other a muscle cell. The path they take depends upon the environment of the cell, including the cells that surround it.

Talking about the isolated individual makes no sense ecologically, because the individual is defined in large part by its environment (Cobb and Birch 1981, chap. 1; Augros and Stanciu 1987, p. 230). Some species may adapt physically to changes in environmental conditions. Certain animals can change food sources as they discover new opportunities.[2] Other organisms may not adapt so easily, or at all. Individual animals may act one way in isolation and another way in a group. Understanding the behavior of a wild individual chimpanzee or bee, for example, may prove difficult if one does not understand where it fits into its population, or society. Species depend upon one another. If it were not for the few species of algae, fungi, and bacteria that fix nitrogen from the atmosphere, soil nitrogen would soon be depleted, and many creatures, including humans, would starve. In many ways, an individual (cell, plant, species) is what it is because of the multitude of relationships it has with the external world. Physical, chemical, social, and psychological pressures force it to adjust if it is to survive and prosper.

Human individuals consist, to a large degree, of the relationships they presently have or have had in the past, combined with the effects of others' interactions. Each person, of course, results from the relationship between his or her father and mother. The stimuli the home environment provides affect his or her physical, mental, and emotional development. The culture into which he or she was born explains to him or her the way the world works and the meaning of life. It defines for each person his or her place in society and the larger world. People know him or her as "the child of George Thorpe," the one who coaches Little League baseball and comes from the East Side. His or her culture filters or interprets his or her sensory experiences, partly determining his or her perception of reality. It tells each person what to expect to see and how the world works (Bandler and Grinder 1975, chap. 1). His or her natural environment may have coevolved with his or her culture—the environment having shaped the culture and the culture having affected the environment.[3] In many ways we are the sum of our past experiences and those of our forebears, and of our individual, unique interpretations of those events. We are part of one another by virtue of our strong effects on one another and our interdependence.[4]

Given that relationships matter, what sorts of relationships tend to predominate in nature? Does the dog-eat-dog competitive model best characterize what we observe, or do cooperation and harmony?

In the past, ecologists have tended to view relationships between species in terms of the struggle for survival. Darwin wrote that "all organic beings are exposed to severe competition" and to "the universal struggle for life due to the pressure of unlimited population growth on limited resources'' (Darwin 1872, rpt. 1958; cited in Augros and Stanciu 1987, p. 89). This perception dominates much of Western thinking about life in general, having given rise, for example, to the expression that "it's a jungle out there."

Many ecologists no longer accept this point of view. As they have studied food webs (the flow of nutrients as they pass through various plant and animal species), they have discovered more and more mutually beneficial partnerships and other types of relationships (Odum 1989, p. 95). Today ecologists tend to see three types of relationships between organisms: competition, complementarity, and supplementarity. Organisms can compete over the same resource. Complementary relationships exist when two organisms live in the same area without directly affecting one another. They neither compete with each other nor help each other. They have a neutral relationship. In supplementary (mutualistic) relationships, organisms aid one another.[5]

Many species avoid competing over resources by occupying different niches within the same habitat. One animal species grazes on leaves in the upper story (canopy) of trees, another species specializes in the middle zone, and yet another focuses on leaves that can be reached from the ground. Or, they eat different parts of the tree—some eat leaves, others eat nectar, others eat fruits. Some animals search for food during the day, others at night. Others migrate during certain seasons, thereby escaping struggles over scarce resources. Plant species do not migrate except in geologic timescales; they can flower, however, at different times to avoid competing for the same pollinators. Or they coevolve with a specific pollinator so that the beak of a certain hummingbird, for example, only fits the flowers of a particular tree (Augros and Stanciu 1987, chap. 4). Thus, many species coexist, rather than struggle, with one another.

Even predator-prey relationships do not fit the picture we often portray of bloody rivalry between two strong heroes (or heroines) of two different species (the noble stag versus the fierce lion). Rather, the predator does not hate or get angry with its prey. It kills to eat, just as we kill chickens for dinner. Few species kill wantonly. Predators generally eat the old, young, and infirm. Consequently, there is little struggle. Even pain is minimized, since the prey often enters shock before death (Augros and Stanciu 1987, chap. 4).

Species cooperate with each other and examples of mutualism abound. Organisms provide shelter, protection, pest control, transportation, and necessary preconditions for survival. Certain ant species live in nodes in tropical *Acacia* trees, receiving shelter in return for protecting the tree from predators. Other ants farm fungi. Honeyguide birds and the badgerlike ratels work together in raiding beehives. Whales carry barnacles around the ocean. Bats eat the fruit of trees and disperse their seeds. Crabs remove ticks from iguanas in the Galápagos (Augros and Stanciu 1987, chap. 4).[6]

Finally, even within species, individuals cooperate. Individuals of some species disperse themselves to avoid competing with one another, for example, by defining territories that are defended by stereotyped displays that rarely result in injury. Or they use dominance hierarchies, or pecking orders, that keep aggression over resources and mates to a minimum (Augros and Stanciu 1987, chap. 4). Herds, flocks, and animal families have strong cooperative behaviors that easily can be described as societies having their own rules and cultures.[7]

Not all biologists agree on the relative importance of competition versus cooperation. However, the above points to the fact that far more cooperation exists in nature than we previously had thought. Perhaps Eugene Odum offers the middle ground: "Contrary to what many people think, nature is not all 'dog-eat-dog.' Competition and predation have their place, but survival often depends on cooperation" (Odum 1989, p. 95). Certainly, interdependence has become evident, as Lewis Thomas, a biologist, states.

A century ago there was a consensus about this: nature was "red in tooth and claw," evolution was a record of open warfare among competing species, the fittest were the strongest aggressors, and so forth. Now it begins to look different. . . . The urge to form partnerships, to link up in collaborative arrangements, is perhaps the oldest, strongest, and most fundamental force in nature. There are no solitary, free-living creatures, every form of life is dependent on other forms. (Thomas 1980, p. 1; cited in Augros and Stanciu 1987, p. 118)

Some scientists now believe that humans not only rely on plants and animals for survival, but they also possess an innate, genetic, emotional attraction to other forms of life. Humans consistently domesticate animals for pets. In the United States zoos attract more visitors than sports events do. The "biophilia hypothesis," first proposed by E. O. Wilson, sees all animals as our kin. All higher organisms are thought to have descended from a single ancestral population approximately 1.8 billion years ago (Kellert 1993, p. 39). Consequently, the hypothesis states that we love other forms of life because we are predisposed genetically to do so. This hypothesis has galvanized a number of scholars to begin exploring it in various ways.

As Wilson has suggested . . . the object of this quest is no less than the possible truth that ''we are human in good part because of the particular way we affiliate with other organisms'' and, more broadly, nature. A central element of this effort has been the belief that the natural environment is critical to human meaning and fulfillment at both the individual and the societal level. (Kellert 1993, p. 25)

Humans live within the natural order, as an integral part of it.[8] Yet, the fact that we can alter our environment far more than any other creature distinguishes us, perhaps, most greatly from any other species. Whereas beaver, for instance, change their habitat by converting stream bottoms into ponds, we can convert entire regions into nuclear wastelands. Although cooperation, or competition limited by substantial cooperation, may characterize the rest of the natural order, Western humanity, at least, wishes to dominate and mold creation to suit its purposes. Whereas predators tend to kill only to eat—they limit their exploitation of other resources—Western humanity appears to place no limit on its exploitation of resources. Does such behavior ultimately strike at the root of human development, at what it means to be human? Does human welfare, physical needs aside, really depend upon the well-being of other creatures? The next chapters address these questions. So, we will leave them for now and turn our attention instead to ecosystems.

The Nature of Ecosystems

Ecosystems resemble solar-powered, multiproduct factories.[9] Any factory requires inputs of energy and raw materials to function. Using the factory building, machinery, and human effort, the factory transforms these inputs into one product, chairs, for instance, or into many outputs, such as chairs, cabinets, tables, and bedsteads. Factories give off waste heat and matter as the result of their production process. Multiproduct ecosystems do the same. Via the process of photosynthesis and the food chain, the plants and animals of the forest transform sunlight (energy) and matter (nutrients and water) into plant and animal biomass of many different kinds. Plants convert sunlight, water, and nutrients from the soil into plant matter that animals then convert into animal tissue. As plants and animals die, fungi and bacteria recycle this biomass into nutrients useful to plants. These processes give off unused matter and energy. The more mature the system, the less it ''wastes'' because the system develops greater capacity to store nutrients for future use.

Ecosystems develop and grow. If humans clear a forest to make a field, species well suited to colonizing such fields (species such as grasses, shrubs, and pioneer trees) move in. They allocate much energy to reproducing quickly and rapidly increase the amount of biomass in the system. During this time, species populations can fluctuate greatly. Over time, new species enter the field as conditions become more propitious for them. As the area becomes more crowded, species with greater capacities for utilizing scarce resources (species that tend to be more specialized in exploiting certain niches) start to dominate. These species may allocate more energy to the adult's survival in a more difficult world (of greater competition for resources) than to reproduction. Biomass grows more slowly now. Whereas more nutrients tended to escape the system in early stages, the more mature system captures far more and experiences less-pronounced population fluctuations. So, during early stages of development, ecosystems tend to produce biomass quickly and experience rapid population shifts, whereas during the more stable, later stages biomass grows slowly (Ewel 1986; Dover and Talbot 1987; Odum 1989).[10]

Ecosystems produce a mix of goods and services, the composition of which can vary. Mangrove forests, for instance, provide wood for construction, poles, and charcoal production; leaves for cattle fodder; nursery facilities for shrimp and deep-water and estuarine fish; habitat for crabs and mollusks; protection against floods, winds, and shore erosion; and retention of sediments, nutrients, and toxic chemicals that enter the estuary or ocean from rivers and streams (Hamilton and Snedaker 1984; de Groot 1986; Larson, et al. 1988; Bell 1989; Gottfried 1992).[11]

Depending upon the way humans use ecosystems, the mix of goods and services changes. Trade-offs and joint production may exist between the various goods and services. As the output of one good or service increases, the quantities produced of other goods and services may rise or fall, thereby changing the output mix. For instance, when wetlands are used to treat human sewage by converting the nutrients into biomass, increased use of this ''nutrient retention service'' leads to more biomass and, possibly, less fish production. When erosion increases in upstream watersheds, downstream wetlands capture more of that sediment, thereby protecting bays from silting up. The wetland produces more sediment retention. As a result, wetland biomass may grow more or less, depending upon the type of wetland and the amount of sediment entering the system. The concentration of sediment in the water, however, affects animal life in the wetland. So, just as in a factory where increased output of one product may imply producing more or less of other outputs, increasing the production of one (or more) goods or services in an ecosystem may lead to more or less of others (Gottfried 1992).[12]

Whereas we often like to think of ecosystems as unchanging (the "balance of nature"), in reality they fluctuate greatly. Change occurs subtly, however, unless the ecosystem is disturbed substantially by some outside force, such as a hurricane or heavy pollution. Checks and balances exist within the system to help regulate it, to keep change within bounds (homeostasis). For instance, the level of photosynthesis of a forest or field varies less than the level of photosynthesis of individual leaves or plants. As photosynthesis falls for one plant, other plants may increase their rate of photosynthesis, thereby compensating for the first plant's decline (Odum 1989, p. 31).

Numerous studies show that ecosystems may have several stable states or conditions. Consider a plaster of paris surface characterized by numerous depressions, hills, and valleys. A ball placed in one of the depressions will stay there when someone moves the surface slightly. However, as she disturbs it more and more forcefully, at some point the ball will rock out of the depression, travel down a valley, and come to rest at a new point. In the new location the ball may be more or less susceptible to disturbances than before. If the new location is very shallow, only a little force may cause it to move elsewhere. Should it move into a deep hole, it may never leave. Should the ball come to the edge of a cliff, it may respond drastically to disturbance by falling off, dramatically changing state.

This implies that, when humans disturb a system, by changing harvesting rates of a fishery or cattle-stocking rates on a pasture, the system may undergo sudden dramatic, and sometimes unexpected, changes. Once-abundant fisheries may collapse. Pastures may experience discontinuous changes in vegetation or insect outbreaks. A cleared tropical-mountain rain forest may come back as pines. Once a system crosses a disturbance threshold, humans may find it difficult to return the system to its original state. Such changes may be irreversible in human time-scales. These state changes may occur far away in space and time from the initial disturbance. For instance, the United States is experiencing declines in its songbird populations as deforestation in Central and South America destroys the birds' winter habitat (May 1977; Holling 1978; Bernstein 1981; Forman and Godron 1986; Dover and Talbot 1987; Scheffer 1990).[13]

Ecologists describe the stability of ecosystems in terms of three characteristics: *persistence* (the constancy of the system over time, as in a nondeclining production or stock of biomass), *resistance* (the system's ability to withstand change), and *resilience* (the capacity to recover from disturbance). Using the above example, when the ball stays in place, the ball persists. When it rolls back to its original location, it demonstrates resilience. When it is so firmly entrenched in a hole that it is hard to move, it resists change.

Ecologists focus on the role of biodiversity in promoting the latter two types of stability. The role of biodiversity in increasing resistance remains highly controversial. It appears more likely that diversity may play a role in fostering resilience. When conditions change, becoming unfavorable to a species that dominates the system, species that are better adapted to the new conditions increase in number and take up the vital roles played by the formerly dominant species. Should a disease wipe out the dominant species, the presence of several others that can play the same role ensures that the key ecological functions played by the dominant species will be fulfilled. Greater species diversity increases the probability that a species in the system will be well suited for the new conditions (Odum 1989, pp. 53, 58). Other ecologists emphasize that stability depends more upon which components are connected to what other components, and the strength of connections between various components and subsystems (Holling 1978; Bernstein 1981; Forman and Godron 1986; Dover and Talbot 1987).

The existence of thresholds implies that there are limits to the amount of change humans can impose on ecosystems without serious, irreversible consequences. The idea of carrying capacity similarly implies limits. Biologists generally talk about two types of carrying capacity: maximum or subsistence capacity and optimum or safe capacity. The former refers to the number of organisms, or amount of biomass, a habitat can support. The latter, a lower number, gives the density of individuals that can live in a habitat with more secure access to food, resistance to predators, and freedom from periodic fluctuations in resources. Because the extent to which humans exploit resources and affect their habitat varies widely, scientists understand that as humans use resources more intensely, carrying capacity falls, and vice versa (Odum 1989, pp. 158–59).

Altering the flows of inputs and outputs of an ecosystem, then, results in ecological consequences. Should humans attempt to keep ecosystems at early stages of development (as when they maintain open fields of annual plants—open-field agriculture—within wooded areas), they must expend energy in weeding to resist the system's tendency to return to woody biomass. When they remove too much biomass from the system (as in some types of tree or crop harvesting), leaving little to be recycled into the nutrient pool available to plants, humans endanger the persistence of biomass production, one of the most valued functions of ecosystems. When they use one function of an ecosystem greatly, they affect the amount and mix of other goods and services they receive.

When humans manage ecosystems by changing their structure, as in modern agriculture and forest plantations, the systems depend upon human-produced inputs such as fertilizer, pesticides, and fossil fuel to maintain themselves. Without these inputs, the systems revert to more natural, often more complex, structures. More natural ecosystems whose structures remain relatively intact do not require human intervention—they maintain and repair themselves. Can humans find ways to minimize the necessity of intervening in ecosystems, while still obtaining valued outputs and minimizing environmental disruption? We will return to that question in chapter 6.

The Importance of Scale

We have seen that ecologists study interactions at various scales, and that we can view even genetic phenomena ecologically. Many phenomena exhibit scale sensitivity; that is, one cannot understand the behaviors or processes at one level without understanding how the next level affects them. One often cannot predict how a group of components will interact by examining them in isolation from one another. Who would think that combining two gases, hydrogen and oxygen, would result in a liquid? Or, who would expect fungi and tree roots to cooperate, producing an efficient method for extracting nutrients from the soil? Scientists call those properties of a system that cannot be predicted from a knowledge of the components of a system ''emergent properties''— properties that emerge at a higher scale.[14]

With the advent of remote sensing from satellites, ecologists have been able to see entire landscapes and examine their ecological processes. For people concerned with land issues, the relatively new field of landscape ecology offers many insights.

Landscape ecologists talk in terms of mosaics. They view the landscape as a patchwork quilt made up of patches of different kinds of habitats, such as forest, fields, wetlands, and urban areas. The sizes, shapes, numbers, kinds, and configurations of the component ecosystems play key roles in affecting ecological processes, and consequently, the goods and services provided by the landscape.[15]

Consider, for example, an isolated patch of forest surrounded by a clear-cut. Many plant and animal species require a certain amount of interior forest, forest that lies a minimum distance away from cleared land. When the size of the forest patch is small, no interior forest exists. The surrounding clear-cut exercises a sufficiently strong influence on the trees of the forest patch that interior species cannot survive. In the case of Douglas-fir forests of the Pacific Northwest of the United States, for instance, the forest and surrounding clear-cuts have different microclimates. Recent studies have shown that the relative humidity and wind of the clear-cut microclimate extend from two hundred to three hundred meters into old growth forest. This means that attaining significant amounts of forest interior in this region requires forest patch sizes of fifty hectares or more. Most forest managers of these forests, however, use patch sizes of ten to fifteen hectares (Franklin 1992). Thus, it matters a great deal ecologically if a forester intending to clear 50 percent of an area does so in one large block or numerous small ones. The former leaves a large, intact area of forest interior whereas the latter fragmented forest does not. Of course, large clear-cuts offer their own problems.

Spatial characteristics of a landscape greatly affect ecological processes. The degree to which patches of different habitat types are connected has an important impact on the persistence of species over time. Hedgerows and fence lines provide protected travel routes for birds and small mammals across fields from one woodlot to another. If woodlots are connected by these corridors, should an animal species become extinct in one woodlot, populations from other woodlots easily can recolonize it. However, should woodlots stand isolated from one another, populations in one woodlot will have difficulty arriving at "empty" woodlots to recolonize them. Roads often fragment habitats, creating disconnected patches. Grizzly bears, for instance, frequent habitats within one hundred meters of a road far less than other habitats. Road development in a 274-square-kilometer area of grizzly habitat in the Rocky Mountains significantly reduced habitat by fragmenting the landscape (Turner 1989). Similarly, the shape of patch can affect species distribution, population stability, and dispersal (Forman and Godron 1986). Round patches of a given area may offer more interior than irregular patches having many arms and intrusions. Irregular patches have much more edge, a factor that favors species that like to move between forest and field, for instance. Spatial patterns also affect other processes such as the flow of nutrients or sediment in surface waters, the flux of gases between the atmosphere and living organisms, and the distribution of nutrients across the landscape (Turner 1989).

The importance of spatial patterns in determining the mix of goods and services gives rise to an emergent property in the economic system: "economies of configuration" (Gottfried, Wear, and Lee 1994). As people on a landscape change its spatial patterns by their decisions on how to use their land, they change the mix of goods and services provided by the landscape. Any one piece of land performs certain ecological functions and provides a certain mix of goods and services, depending upon the spatial configuration of patches on the surrounding landscape. The owner of that piece of land, or its manager, thus faces a given configuration of the landscape. However, all the landowners together determine the landscape configuration, and therefore the ecological functions provided by each piece of land. For example, a strip of forest land next to a river plays an important role in preventing erosion from entering the stream. The trees, shrubs, and grass trap sediment flowing down the hillsides, thereby protecting water quality. If that strip lies within a large patch of forest, it may provide little sediment retention because little sediment reaches it. However, if that strip borders a large clear-cut, the strip may play a critical role in protecting water quality. What any one piece of land or habitat patch does, then, depends upon the spatial pattern of the landscape. The landscape's output depends upon its configuration.

At the level of the planet, some scientists suggest that even other emergent properties operate. Lovelock (1982) asserts that the biosphere regulates itself, that the living organisms in the biosphere play the dominant role in maintaining the earth as a livable habitat. The relatively stable temperature of the earth and salinity of ocean waters over time, proponents say, occur because of the interaction of living organisms with their nonliving environment. Debate over this "Gaia hypothesis" has been, and continues to be, intense.[16] Part of the difficulty of the hypothesis lies in the difficulty of testing it. The most radical version of the Gaia hypothesis states that the minds of people in some way intimately interrelate with, and control, the earth. The biosphere now resembles an organism with a mind.

Without attempting to judge the validity of the Gaia hypothesis, we can ask whether some principles may emerge at the biospheric level that we cannot deduce from our perspective. Are we constrained from seeing processes that emerge at a higher level by our being components of the biosphere? If we were a mind transcending the biosphere, would we perceive processes that finite humans limited by their scale of analysis cannot?

We have seen that we depend upon our natural environment and form it. Our environment, in turn, forms us. As part of the community of life, we live in a natural world characterized by much cooperation. Can humans, therefore, attempt to dominate nature with impunity? Should we dominate it, or should we, too, attempt to cooperate with nature and its processes? Do we become less human by dominating nature? Can we fully understand the mechanisms that affect our answer, or do we confront problems of scale?

We can approach these questions in two ways. First, we can examine the social and ecological processes that affect human well-being, as well as the well-being of other creatures. Second, we can address the ethical-moral dimension implicit in our questions. In this chapter we already have laid the ecological framework for our first approach. We will continue working on the first approach in chapters 5, 6 and 7. However, before we proceed further we need to consider the moral dimension.

Because Western tradition in many ways has roots in the Hebrew civilization at the beginning of the Common Era, the time of the birth of Christ, Westerners probably should begin there for values with which to answer ethical questions. We will find that civilization offers surprising answers to our questions about the nature of humanity's relationship to its natural environment, the effects of the human domination of nature, and the question of scale.

For millennia people have rearranged ecosystems on small scales—gardens—in order to feed themselves. In comparison, societies garden at the landscape or greater level, structuring natural systems consciously or unconsciously to suit societal purposes. Because very few places today escape the human touch directly or indirectly, we now can treat the entire earth as one garden. Accordingly, let us begin our exploration with one of the oldest and most powerful images in Western tradition, the Garden.

Notes

1. To understand the role of structure on behavior, consider the following experiment. Tie a small rock onto a two-foot string and tie the string to a branch several feet above the ground. Hold the rock in your outstretched hand and hold it in front of you. Let go. What happens? Now take a large, flexible spring and

tie the rock onto one end. Attach the other to the branch. Now hold this rock in your hand so that the spring is not stretched at all. Let go. What happens? In the first case, letting go causes the rock to fall until it comes to a quick stop. In the second case, letting go causes the rock to fall and then oscillate up and down. The same action causes two different behaviors. The difference lies in the structure of each system. System structures, therefore, determine behavior.

2. Consider the famous case of the tits, a species of bird, in Great Britain. One tit discovered that it could pierce the caps on bottles of milk delivered and left outside homes. Soon tits all over England became milk bottle feeders, something they had not been before.

3. Many animal and plant species have coevolved, becoming totally dependent upon one another. For instance, certain trees depend upon specific birds or bats to pollinate their flowers, and those pollinators evolve to depend upon those specific tree species for food. Both species can become so interdependent that, should one be eliminated, the other cannot survive. Similarly, human cultures may coevolve with their natural environment. Native peoples burn off fields, domesticate or exterminate plants and animals, and change the spatial distribution of plants, thereby influencing their environment. Their environment affects their culture, and cultures often evolve in ways that limit ecologically unsound behavior. Taboos against certain practices often protect delicate ecosystems from being overexploited. Those same individuals, placed in another context, would have developed a different culture in response to the challenges posed by their environment. The human and ecological systems, therefore, strongly influence each other's character.

4. This does not imply environmental determinism. Individuals react differently to the same experiences. Two identical twins witnessing the same fight may interpret the motivations for the fight entirely differently. People have their own sets of mental constructs with which they interpret the world, in addition to the cultural constructs given to them by society (Bandler and Grinder 1975, chap. 1). So, while the environment, both human and natural, greatly affects an individual, the individual still possesses unique characteristics.

The case of the cowboy may help make the point. In the frontier days of the United States, judges hanged horse thieves because people depended so greatly upon their horses. Because people depended upon their horses so much, stealing a person's horse greatly jeopardized a person's well-being, even to the point of condemning the former owner to death. While two distinct organisms, the cowboy depended upon his horse so thoroughly that a person could not totally distinguish one from the other. The horse enabled the cowboy to be who he was. No horse, no cowboy.

Meeks points out that, in Christian theology, the Creator is not an individual but a community. The doctrine of the Trinity states that this community consists of three distinct persons, each with its own characteristics and tasks. Yet, according to the ancient Cappadocian doctrine of "mutual coinherence," their relationships with one another make them who they are. They become totally one, totally unified, by virtue of their perfect othercenteredness, their perfect self-giving to one another. They totally form, or interpenetrate, one another. This community serves as a model for the type of human relationships the Creator intends (Meeks 1989, pp. 11–12; see also Maloney 1979).

5. Thanks to Sarah Warren, a forest ecologist, for bringing these three categories of relationships to my attention.

6. Dryzek (1987, p. 233) points out that recent work in evolutionary biology suggests that species strategies having large components of cooperation may possess high survival value.

7. For a fascinating, enjoyable book describing relationships between species in the tropics of the New World, see Kricher (1989).

8. Although many top-rank ecologists such as Eugene Odum, one of the great modern figures in ecology, agree with this statement, a significant number of ecologists appear to feel otherwise. Of course, the scale of analysis matters. When one examines nutrient cycling in undisturbed sites, humans play no role. However, in this author's view, many ecologists prefer to study nature as it would be without humans; i.e., in a "natural" state, failing to take into account that, in many ways, humans have influenced greatly the character of apparently "natural" systems they are studying. Humans are animals. Most scientists believe that we descended from a primate ancestor via natural processes. We depend upon natural processes just as others do. Consequently, as much as we may dislike the results of human behavior, (in this author's opinion) to say that humans do not fit within the natural order appears rather ingenuous and unscientific.

9. I avoid the controversy in ecological and economic circles over energetics. Howard Odum and many other ecologists view energy flows as the foundation of any ecological understanding. Some, including Odum, then go on to analyze economic and other social phenomena in the same way. Needless to say, many economists have difficulty with this approach, seeing it as reductionistic. While such an approach may offer substantial insights, the thesis of this book does not require such an analysis. So, I leave it to interested readers to follow it on their own. See Odum and Odum (1981) for a good introduction to the subject.

10. This presents challenges for humans who want agricultural systems that are both productive and stable. Colinvaux states that a three-strategy model tends to fit plant succession data better than the two-strategy model used above. First, "colonizers"—well adapted to invading areas with little competition and reproducing rapidly in the new area—move in. They are adapted to frequent disturbance but not competition for scarce resources. Then "competitor" species adapted to low disturbance and low stress move in, maintaining dense populations and replacing colonizers over time. Finally, "stress competitors"—species adapted to low disturbance and intense competition over resources (stress)—move in, gradually replacing the competitors (Colinvaux 1986, pp. 588–89).

Ecosystem development also may provide insight into how to trap carbon to prevent global warming. When ecosystems quickly add biomass, they trap large quantities of carbon that otherwise would remain in the atmosphere in the form of carbon dioxide. Mature ecosystems, however, take in and give off roughly comparable amounts of carbon dioxide. Less-mature ecosystems, therefore, may provide greater carbon sequestration services than more mature natural systems.

11. Mangrove forests exist in subtropical and tropical areas like Florida and Central America. They tolerate salt water. Therefore, they can live in the intertidal zone where few other plants can survive. One common species has aerial roots that extend down from the branches into the water, forming, along with the actual roots of the tree, a tangled web difficult to penetrate.

12. The interest in the economic importance of ecosystems, particularly wetlands, has stimulated a fascinating literature on their economic value. For an introduction to the literature, see Gosselink et al. (1973); Foster (1979); Batie and Shabman (1982); Bell (1989); Costanza et al. (1989); Freeman (1991); and Gottfried (1992).

13. Some theoretical models indicate that as more species are added to a system, more and more hills and valleys emerge—the ecosystem gains more stable states (May 1977, p. 477).

14. Prices demonstrate the importance of scale phenomena in economics. In a competitive market system, individuals cannot influence prices. They take prices as given, as part of their environment. However, all individuals together do determine the level of prices and their movements. Price determination emerges at the market level.

15. See (Ewel 1986; Forman and Godron 1986; Turner 1989; Franklin 1992; Lee et al. 1992; Stanford and Ward 1992; Naveh and Lieberman 1993) for discussions of spatial patterns on ecological processes.

16. The Greeks named their earth goddess "Gaia."

References

Augros, Robert, and George Stanciu. 1987. *The New Biology: Discovering the Wisdom in Nature.* Boston: Shambala.

Bandler, R., and J. Grinder. 1975. *The Structure of Magic.* Palo Alto: California Science and Behavior Books.

Batie, Sandra S., and Leonard A. Shabman. 1982. "Estimating the Economic Value of Wetlands: Principles, Methods, and Limitations." *Coastal Zone Management Journal* 10(3): 255–78.

Bell, Frederick W. 1989. "Application of Wetland Valuation Theory to Florida Fisheries." Florida Sea Grant Program, 95 (June). Florida Sea Grant College.

Bernstein, Brock. 1981. "Ecology and Economics: Complex Systems in

Changing Environments." *Annual Review of Ecology and Systematics* 12: 309–30.

Cobb, John B., Jr., and Charles Birch. 1981. *The Liberation of Life: From the Cell to the Community.* New York: Cambridge University Press.

Colinvaux, Paul. 1986. *Ecology.* New York: John Wiley & Sons.

Costanza, Robert, Stephen C. Farber, and Judith Maxwell. 1989. "The Valuation and Management of Wetland Ecosystems." *Ecological Economics* 1(4): 335–61.

Darwin, Charles. 1872; rpt. 1958. *The Origin of Species.* London; rpt. New York: Norton.

de Groot, R. S. 1986. "A Functional Ecosystem Evaluation Method as a Tool in Environmental Planning and Decision Making." Unpublished paper. Nature Conservation Department, Agricultural University, Wageningen, The Netherlands.

Dover, Michael, and Lee M. Talbot. 1987. *To Feed the Earth: Agro-Ecology for Sustainable Development.* Washington DC: World Resources Institute.

Dryzek, John. 1987. *Rational Ecology: Environment and Political Economy.* New York: Basil Blackwell.

Ewel, John J. 1986. "Designing Agricultural Ecosystems for the Humid Tropics." *Annual Review of Ecology and Systematics* 17: 245–71.

Forman, Richard T., and Michel Godron. 1986. *Landscape Ecology.* New York: John Wiley and Sons.

Foster, John H. 1979. "Measuring the Social Value of Wetland Benefits." In *Wetland Functions and Values: The State of Our Understanding: Proceedings of the National Symposium on Wetlands Held in Disneyworld Village, Lake Buena Vista, Florida, November 7–10, 1978,* ed. Phillip Greeson, John Clark, and Judith Clark. Minneapolis: American Water Resources Association.

Franklin, Jerry F. 1992. "Scientific Basis for New Perspectives in Forests and Streams." In *Watershed Management: Balancing Sustainability and Environmental Change,* ed. Robert J. Naiman. New York: Springer-Verlag.

Freeman, A. Myrick, III. 1991. "Valuing Environmental Resources under Alternative Management Regimes." *Ecological Economics* 3(3): 247–56.

Gosselink, James G., Eugene P. Odum, and R. M. Pope. 1973. "The Value of the Tidal Marsh." (May 1). Urban and Regional Development Center, University of Florida, Gainesville.

Gottfried, Robert. 1992. "The Value of a Watershed as a Series of Linked Multiproduct Assets." *Ecological Economics* 5: 145–61.

Gottfried, Robert, David Wear, and Robert Lee. 1994. "Landscapes, Ecosystem Value, and Sustainability." Paper presented at the 1994 Association of Environmental and Resource Economists Workshop, "Integrating the Environment and the Economy: Sustainable Development and Economic/Ecological Modeling," June 6, at Boulder, Colo.

Hamilton, Lawrence S., and Samuel C. Snedaker. 1984. "Handbook for Mangrove Area Mangement." Honolulu: United Nations Environment Programme and East-West Center, Environment and Policy Institute.

Holling, C. S. 1978. "The Nature and Behavior of Ecological Systems." Pp. 25–37 in *Adaptive Environmental Assessment and Management*, ed. C. S. Holling. New York: John Wiley and Sons.

Kellert, Stephen R. 1993. "Introduction." Pp. 20–27 in *The Biophilia Hypothesis*, ed. Stephen R. Kellert, and Edward O. Wilson. Washington, DC: Island Press.

Kricher, John. 1989. *A Neotropical Companion: An Introduction to the Animals, Plants, and Ecosystems of the New World Tropics*. Princeton, NJ: Princeton University Press.

Larson, Joseph S., Paul R. Adamus, and Ellis J. Clairain, Jr. 1988. "Functional Assessment of Freshwater Wetlands: A Manual and Training Outline." Unpublished. (June).

Lee, Robert G., Richard Flamm, Monica G. Turner, et al. 1992. "Integrating Sustainable Development and Environmental Vitality: A Landscape Ecology Approach." In *Watershed Management. Balancing Sustainability and Environmental Change*, ed. Robert J. Naiman. New York: Springer-Verlag.

Lovelock, J. E. 1982. *Gaia: A New Look at Life on Earth*. New York: Oxford University Press.

Maloney, George A. 1979. *Invaded by God: Mysticism and the Indwelling Trinity*. Denville, NJ: Dimension Books.

May, R. 1977. "Thresholds and Breakpoints in Ecosystems with a Multiplicity of Stable States." *Nature* 269: 471–77.

Meeks, M. Douglas. 1989. *God the Economist: The Doctrine of God and Political Economy*. Minneapolis: Fortress Press.

Naveh, Zev, and Arthur Lieberman. 1993. *Landscape Ecology: Theory and Application*. New York: Springer-Verlag.

Odum, Eugene. 1989. *Ecology and Our Endangered Life-Support Systems*. Stamford, CT: Sinauer.

Odum, Howard T., and Elisabeth C. Odum. 1981. *Energy Basis for Man and Nature*. New York: McGraw-Hill.

Scheffer, Marten. 1990. "Multiplicity of Stable States in Fresh Water Systems." *Hydrobiologia* 200/201: 475–86.

Stanford, J. A., and J. V. Ward. 1992. "Management of Aquatic Resources in Large Catchments: Recognizing Interactions Between Ecosystem Connectivity and Environmental Disturbance." In *Watershed Management. Balancing Sustainability and Environmental Change*, ed. Robert J. Naiman. New York: Springer-Verlag.

Thomas, Lewis. 1980. "On the Uncertainty of Science." *Phi Beta Kappa Key Reporter* 6:1.

Turner, Monica Goigel. 1989. "Landscape Ecology: The Effect of Pattern on Process." *Annual Review of Ecology and Systematics* 20: 171–97.

Woodmansee, R. G. 1990. "Biogeochemical Cycles and Ecological Hierarchies." Pp. 57–71 in *Changing Landscapes: An Ecological Perspective*, ed. I. S. Zonneveld, and R. T. T. Forman. New York: Springer-Verlag.

Chapter 3

On Roots: The Nature of Nature

To understand how the Jewish civilization at the beginning of the Common Era understood the relationship between people and nature, we need to change our vocabulary. The Jewish culture did not distinguish between them. In fact, it had no word for nature separate from humanity (Gregorios 1987, p. 87).[1]

Nature as Creation

We in the West tend to view the world from an anthropocentric view. Humans form the center of the world, so that we view everything around us from the human perspective: certain animals threaten us, particular plants yield beautiful flowers, rivers flood our homes. The Jews saw the world theocentrically. Everything revolved around the great One who made all things and shepherded the Hebrew people.

Consequently, when the Jews spoke of "nature," they used the word *beriah*, or "creating." This word implied, first, that only two categories exist in the world—the Creator and that which the Creator fashions. So, humans, animals, plants, and rocks all belong to the same category: creation. Second, *beriah* expresses the view that all of creation is an ongoing created order reflecting dynamism and change (Gregorios 1987; Rasmussen 1987). Creation is not a one-time event. Rather, the Creator constantly makes the creation. According to Walter Brueggemann (1977, p. 15), the central vision of world history in the Jewish writings is that "all creation is one, every creature in community with every other, living in harmony and security toward the joy and well-being of every other creature." Creation consists of a vast public household, or *oikos* (a Greek word for "household"), the latter being the root

29

for the words "economics," "ecology," and "ecumenism."[2] In the ancient Near East, including Israel, "creation" unifies the cosmic, political and social orders in one concept (Schmid 1973, p. 105).

This vast creation belongs to the One who invited it into being. As Psalms 24:1–2 declares,

> The earth is the Lord's and all that is in it,
> the world, and those who live in it;
> for he has founded it on the seas,
> and established it on the rivers.[3]

According to Genesis 1, the Creator sees all the Creator's work as good, *tob*, or (better translated) as pleasing or beautiful (Tucker 1993, p. 113).

Although various books of the Bible (Genesis 1–11, Psalms, and Isaiah) have creation accounts that some consider anthropocentric, the Book of Job makes it clear that the Creator forms the world "for his own inscrutable pleasure"(Clifford 1988, p. 162). Here the author of the book relates the wonders of creation to teach his readers about the error of an egoistic, anthropocentric approach to creation. While some creatures may be useful to humans, others such as the ostrich and Leviathan, exist only because their creator delights in them (Jb 38:39–39:6).[4] Instead of controlling each creature as a cosmic puppeteer, the Creator allows each creature freedom to be itself (e.g., Jb 39:5). In Job, humanity exists on the periphery of creation, not at its center (Baker 1979, p. 17; Clifford 1988, pp. 162–63).

Because creation is an ongoing process, if the Creator ever stops sustaining the Creator's handiwork, creation ceases to exist. The psalmist, for instance, when speaking about the animals, states that:

> These all look to you to give them their food in due season;
> when you give to them, they gather it up;
> when you open your hand, they are filled with good things.
> When you hide your face, they are dismayed;
> when you take away their breath, they die and return to their dust.
> When you send forth your spirit, they are created;
> and you renew the face of the ground. (Ps 104:27–30)

The belief that the Creator continually fashions and sustains the world provided the cornerstone for Israel's interpretation of its history and the early Christians' understanding of Jesus (Schmid 1973, p. 111). [5]

Creation responds to its faithful, ongoing sustainer. In the Creator's presence the trees of the field "clap their hands." The heavens and earth sing to the Creator—the sea roars, the fields exult, the heavens proclaim their maker's glory (Psalms 19 and 96). The beauty of creation causes all creatures to be joyful, a joy that leads all creatures to praise their maker (Westermann 1982, p. 93). This will occur even more in the future when "the earth will be filled with the knowledge of the glory of the Lord, as waters cover the sea" (Hb 2:14). All beings have the capacity and moral responsibility to respond to the Creator and relate appropriately to others (Austin 1988, pp. 47–49). Humans live in a world that responds enthusiastically to its creator, a world that belongs to the One who made it.[6]

The Nature of Humanity

For the Jewish people, relationships define the individual. "Jane Goodman," for instance, consists of her mannerisms, family background, life experiences, smell, appearance—all those things that make her a unique person. Moreover, her mind, body, and spirit cannot be separated from one another—they form an integrated whole. Thus, when the writers of scripture ask for their souls to be delivered, they mean that they want to be saved from death (Bonifazi 1970, p. 207; Tucker 1993).

We *receive* our being from others rather than *have* being. Our existence depends upon two people having been in relationship with one another. We depend upon the efforts of many people each day who provide us with the necessities, and luxuries, of life. Ultimately we receive our being from the Creator who sustains all those creatures who sustain us. As Hall (1986) says,

> The confession that God is the source and ground of our being is, rather, simultaneously a confession of our dependence on these created "others": the parents who conceived and nurtured us; the siblings whose companionship (and rivalry) shaped our formative years; the friends, co-workers, neighbors, teachers, students, and colleagues with whom we are linked in voluntary or involuntary communality; the dogs and cats whose presence in our childhood and at other times may have been even more significant than that of people; the animals and plants that sustain our bodies and the wine that makes our souls glad; the trees, the particular landscapes, the mountains, the sea, the rivers and prairies; the sun and skies; the ground with which, despite false pride, we have an aboriginal affinity: through each and all of these, creatures though they be, our being has been shaped and is being sustained. I know perfectly well that I would not be who I

have become or am becoming without the quite specific faces that have beamed upon me or scolded and questioned me from my youth up; or the quite particular climate in which I was reared and have lived most of my life (the snow); or the animals I have loved—and who loved me more than I them; or the trees, the splendid trees. (p. 134)

Humans, therefore, do not stand in splendid isolation apart from "nature." Rather, humanity's interrelatedness with all of creation, human and extrahuman, emerges as a key insight of Jewish scriptures.[7]

So far nothing distinguishes humans from any other creature. Yet, the scriptures speak about humans being "a bit lower than God" (Ps 8). Although humanity shares its created nature with everything else that exists, the Creator gives humans a unique role and equips them for that mission. Let us consider, then, the uniqueness of human beings.

The scriptures tell two stories of the creation of humans within the context of a larger creation process.[8] Genesis 1:1–2:3 speaks of humans being created after the creation of the heavens and all other creatures. On the sixth day, the Creator "created humankind in his image, in the image of God he created them; male and female he created them" (Gn 1:27). Genesis 2:4–25 describes a different process whereby the Creator fashioned Adam out of the ground, later fashioning Eve from Adam's rib.

Following the second creation story, the Creator placed Adam in the Garden of Eden "to till and to keep it." After realizing that "it is not good that the man should be alone," the Creator fashioned the animals, which Adam named. Seeing that none of these was a suitable partner for Adam, the Creator made Eve.

This story tells us several things about the nature of humanity. The creation of human life involved not only the moments of creating Adam and Eve, but also the creating of their living space (the Garden), their means of life (the fruits of the Garden), their vocation (to cultivate and care for the Garden), their community (man and woman), and the medium of communication necessary for community (speech). Being human involves, for the writer of Genesis 2, relationships with the Creator, other humans, and the Garden. It implies that the Garden provides the needs of humans who, in turn, care for the Garden (Westermann 1982, pp. 94–95).

Being human carries with it a vocation, a permission, and a prohibition. First, humans must care for and cultivate the Garden. The words used here are *abad* and *shamar*. The former means to serve, even to the point of "being a slave to." The latter, besides meaning "keep," also means to watch or preserve. Humans serve and preserve the Garden, not vice versa. Second, they have permission to eat of any tree for their sustenance. Third, humans live under an authority that constrains their freedom. They may eat no animals. Most importantly, however, they may not eat of the tree of the knowledge of good and evil. Human life involves the struggle of holding these three facets of human existence together (Brueggemann 1983, p. 46; Granberg-Michaelson 1984, p. 65).

The other creation story, in Genesis 1, relates that the Creator made humans in the Creator's image. Because of the temptations of Babylonian religion with its images of deities, Israel determinedly resisted the use of images of the Creator with one exception—humanity itself. Only humans image the Creator, because humans can receive power, make decisions, and honor commitments. Given rule over creation by the Creator, they alone can image a faithful and gracious Creator to creation. Just as kings placed images, or statues, of themselves in remote regions where they themselves could not be present, so the Creator placed an image to represent the Creator on earth and to rule for the Creator (Maly 1968, p. 11; Brueggemann 1983, pp. 31–32).

Representing the Creator before creation requires a being that exists not so much for itself as for others. As Brueggemann points out, creation itself "is God's decision not to look after himself but to focus his energies and purposes on creation" (Brueggemann 1983, p. 34). Hall argues that the "image of God" means that humans exist for relationships. Relatedness-in-love is the essence and vocation of creatures fashioned by a creator who *is* love. To be human is to "be-with" another. To the extent that humans relate lovingly with their creator, with one another, and with extrahuman creation, three inseparably linked dimensions of love, then they present to creation a visible image of their creator (Hall 1986, p. 132).[9]

Similarly, Christian tradition interprets Jesus of Nazareth as the "Image of God" (Col 1:15). As the perfect human, the one willing "to lay down his life for his friends," Jesus reflects the total self-giving of the Creator to creation. The Creator gives (it)self so thoroughly to creation that the Creator becomes human, becoming both creature and Creator. The latter loves creation so thoroughly that the Creator identifies totally with it, becoming one with it (the doctrine of the Incarnation).

Both creation stories, then, declare that humans exist to live in a self-giving relationship with other humans, the rest of creation, and the Creator. By giving themselves totally to others, they serve as a mirror, reflecting the image of the Creator to creation. They thereby make visible an otherwise invisible reality.

The Creator made this reality explicit through many covenants, which made concrete the Creator's desire for intimacy with creation. Biblical covenants consist of legal agreements that express the fundamental relationship between the Jewish people and their Creator (Clifford 1994).[10] Other biblical expressions of covenantal relationship include descriptions of being the Creator's "children" or family; the Creator as father, mother, friend, and lover (Hall 1986, p. 144).

Four covenants in particular reveal the nature of the three-way relationship between Creator, people, and the rest of creation. After the great flood, the scriptures state that the Creator made a covenant between (it)self, Noah (humanity), and all living beings to maintain the natural cycles of creation and to destroy never again the earth by flood (Gen 9:8–17). To underscore the scope of the covenant as extending to all living creatures, the author of the passage repeats five times that the covenant extends to all living things. As a reminder and sign of the covenant, the Creator sets the rainbow, an unstrung bow, in the sky (Granberg-Michaelson 1990, p. 30). In another covenant the Creator promised Abraham that his countless descendants would live in a land set aside for them. Even the covenant with Moses on Mount Sinai encompasses all of creation. As Granberg-Michaelson (1990, p. 30) points out, before giving the Ten Commandments, the Creator reminds Moses that "the whole earth is mine" (Ex 19:5). The same occurs in Deuteronomy's parallel account of these events (10:14). The covenants with Israel always involved land and the Creator (Brueggemann 1977, p. 52).

The prophet Hosea expresses the intimate relationship between the covenant partners. When Israel abandons its worship of the idol Baal and returns to its loving maker,

On that day, says the Lord, you will call me, "My husband," and no longer will you call me, "My Baal." . . . I will make for you a covenant on that day with the wild animals, the birds of the air, and the creeping things of the ground; and I will abolish the bow, the sword, and war from the land; and I will make you lie down in safety. And I will take you for my wife forever; I will take you for my wife in righteousness and in justice, in steadfast love, and in mercy. I will take you for my wife in faithfulness; and you shall know the Lord.

On that day I will answer, says the Lord, I will answer the heavens, and they shall answer the earth; and the earth shall answer the grain, the wine, and the oil, and they shall answer Jezreel [Israel]; and I will sow him for myself in the Land. (Hos 2:16–23)

The three-way covenant makes explicit the understanding from Genesis that humanity has a responsibility to other humans, to the land, and to the Creator. For instance, Noah, the just man, took responsibility for creation by taking two of every animal into the ark so that their species might continue after the Deluge. Because the Creator allowed humans to eat animals only after the Deluge (as a concession to humanity's inherent perversity), Noah's action was purely altruistic (Clifford 1994, p. 6). Similarly, the ancient Jews understood that current generations hold land in trust for future generations. Thus, they cannot trade away an inalienable inheritance. In essence, the "owner" belongs to the land, not vice versa.

As Israel prepared to cross the Jordan to enter the Promised Land, Moses declared that the people should keep the Sabbath every seventh day for a time of rest. Similarly, they would rest the land every seventh year (a Sabbath year). After forty-nine years (seven times seven), the people would experience the jubilee year, a year for freeing slaves, resting the land, and canceling debts. The Sabbaths and jubilee year served as reminders that land is a gift with its own rights.[11] Taking someone's land oppresses not only that person but also the land itself. Because the land should sustain all members of the human community, Moses enjoined Israel to care for the poor, stranger, sojourner, widow, orphan, and Levite (a cultic figure) because they had no land. Ultimately, neither people nor land can be owned or managed because they live together in a covenant relationship with the giver of life (Brueggemann 1977, pp. 65–66, 91, 97–98).

Humanity's potential to mirror the Creator to the Creator's creation and to exercise authority within the covenant to some degree lies most radically in the human capacity for speech. Creation finds a voice in humanity, a creature that can address the Creator. Humankind serves as a mediatorial species that not only reflects the Creator's glory but gives voice to creation's gratitude (Hall, pp. 204–5).

This gift of speech confers the authority to make a difference in the world. Humans have a peculiarly intimate relationship with the Creator who, in Genesis 1, makes a particularly intense commitment to them by speaking directly only to them and by granting them the freedom to respond (Brueggemann 1977, p. 31). Thus, when Adam named the animals, he demonstrated that he shared some of the Creator's insight into the essence of each species, because a name was considered to distill the essence of a being into one word (Baker 1979, p. 11). Because knowing someone's name, and therefore knowing the person, implied having some degree of control over them, Adam also exhibited his superiority and authority over the animals. This did not imply possessive power, however. Adam named his wife, a being given him as a "compatible helper," someone not subordinate and "incompatible" like other animals. Therefore, naming connotes "appropriate authority, affinity and care" (Clifford 1994, p. 8).

Similarly, when the Creator speaks sovereignly, thereby creating the universe, the Creator binds ("it")self in a "distinctive and delicate way" to the creation with which the Creator has a faithful relationship. This binding together of creation and faithful Creator undergirds the entire message of the scriptures (Brueggemann 1983, pp. 22, 24).

Christians identified the words of the Creator at the beginning of the world, the words by which creation was made, with Jesus (Jn 1:1–5). All the old values of the Jewish tradition found a new, personal expression in the Word of the Creator made flesh. The words that he spoke healed, raised the dead, calmed waves, inspired, and carried authority. As the Word, he exemplified how humans were to interact with one another and creation. We speak to one another, and otherwise affect one another, in ways that either make us whole or hurt. Jesus, who unites creation and creator, invites humans to speak and act in healing, compassionate ways.

As humans, we, in essence, create our own environment while we create ourselves. To the extent we truly desire the good of others, know others so that we know what their good would be, and act accordingly, we create wholeness. To the extent that we fail to comprehend others and desire their welfare, we create misery. For this reason we share in the creative activity of the Creator. When our creativity brings more love and beauty into the world, we act as our maker's image. We also bring the image of the Creator more clearly into focus in the world.

The Concept of Dominion

The above discussion of the relationship between humans and the rest of creation conflicts with popular interpretations of Genesis 1:26–28, which enjoins humans to subdue the earth and to have dominion over it. Many Christians and non-Christians believe that these passages give humans the right to exploit creation at will for their benefit. However, believing that humans can exploit creation makes people less than human, as we have come to understand. Moreover, it violates the concept of dominion, which the Bible portrays quite differently from a license to exploit.

When Adam named the animals, he exercised his sovereignty over them. Naming someone not only showed insight into his or her nature, but established a claim over him or her. Parents named their children and overlords named their vassals (Baker 1979, p. 11). However, the Creator, in turn, named Adam, thereby demonstrating that Adam (and Eve) exercised authority as vassals themselves.

Genesis 1:26–28, which speaks about subduing the earth, needs to be understood in context. According to Brueggemann (1977, p. 144; 1983, pp. 22–27), the writers of Genesis 1–2:4a wrote these passages to comfort the sixth-century Jewish exiles in Babylon. Far from the Temple and Promised Land, these people confronted the chaos of uprootedness. The priestly writers of Genesis 1 tried to comfort the exiles and to assure them that their creator maintained control and sovereignty despite appearances. Babylonian gods had not conquered the Jewish Creator. Instead the Creator sustained and ruled over all life.

For this reason the priestly authors used strong language to express dominion and subduing. The word for the former translates more accurately as "trample" and the latter as "tread down" (Maly 1968, p. 11). The Creator tramples the Babylonian nature gods through regents on earth. Peace, however, marks the regent's relationship to the rest of creation. Humans eat only seed-bearing plants and fruits, while animals eat only green plants.

Other authors offer further insight. Granberg-Michaelson (1984, p. 63) notes that humans subjugate the "earth," which literally means the ground, not the world. Humans, who are to eat the plants of the earth, must cultivate the ground for food. This makes eminent sense to the agricultural societies of the day that battled the forces of nature to wrest food from the ground. Clifford points out that filling and subduing the earth relates to each nation's first-time seizure of the land allotted to it by the Creator, as the history described in Genesis 1–11:9 attests (1988, pp. 165–66; 1994, pp. 6–7).

Despite the harsh language, then, humanity's dominion means something other than the way we popularly interpret it. In order to understand dominion, let us turn to the nature of kingship in the Jewish civilization. In the ancient Near East, the king served as a vice-regent for the gods. As one of his main duties he ensured the fertility and prosperity of the kingdom by obeying the gods and observing rituals. The Jews retained this understanding of kingship. As long as the king maintained his relationship with the Creator, his power remained intact and his effective rule over his people and other creatures of his kingdom continued. However, if he strayed, he lost the power given him and prosperity ceased (see the discussion of The Blessing in the next section).

Although the Jewish concept of king shared characteristics common to those of other ancient Near Eastern cultures, the Jews still understood kingship quite differently. The Jewish king had to be a kinsman, not a foreigner. He could not possess a large number of horses lest he use them for war. Neither could he acquire large numbers of wives or precious metals lest these estrange him from his relationship with his creator, in whose name he ruled. In order that the king might live in awe of the Creator and always obey his Lord, he was supposed to read the Torah, or law, all the days of his life (Dt 17:14–20). The prophet Ezekiel declared that the king should be a shepherd who cares for his sheep (Ez 34). Christianity later understood Jesus to be the ultimate king, a ruler identifying totally with his people and willing to give himself totally for them, a shepherd "who lays down his life for his sheep" (Jn 10:11). The king, then, ruled as one of the community, serving them sensitively and caringly.[12]

Kings must act righteously, or justly, toward all. Particularly in Job, faithfulness to the community, or righteousness, went hand in hand with dominion (Koch 1983, p. 81). When the ancient Jews extolled the justice of their creator, they proclaimed that the Creator faithfully maintained the order of creation, keeping chaos at bay, even at the cost of using harsh measures. The king demonstrated justice by enforcing not just strict legal justice, but also by following customs intended to ensure equity, particularly customs regarding the distribution of land. So, justice, *mishpat*, carried the dimensions of righteousness, loving kindness, faithfulness, completeness/integrity, and equity (Foster 1981, pp. 27–28).

The Jews often brought *mishpat* and compassion, *hesed*, intimately together. Scholars often translate *hesed* as "loving-kindness" or "mercy." It includes the ideas of unwavering faithfulness and enduring, everlasting compassion or love. Righteous people, therefore, reflected the steadfast love of the Creator, the Creator's *hesed*. Justice resided not only in acting fairly, but in showing kindness and mercy:

> Thus says the Lord of hosts: Render true judgments, show kindness and mercy to one another; do not oppress the widow, the orphan, the alien, or the poor; and do not devise evil in your hearts against one another (Zec 7: 9–10).

> . . . what does the Lord require of you but to do justice, and to love kindness, and to walk humbly with your God? (Mi 6:8)

The attitude or inner spirit with which people acted mattered greatly, as did right behavior (Foster 1981, pp. 27–28).

Righteousness involved caring for the weak and deprived, including all of creation. Proverbs 12:10, for instance, states that "The righteous know the needs of their animals." Caring for animals represented more than wise business practice—loving kindness required it. Similarly, Deuteronomy 20:19 states that when laying siege to a city, the army may not cut down the trees because they provide food.

In commenting upon this latter passage, the rabbis developed the law of *bal tashhit*, or "do not destroy," which applied to a wide range of environmental regulations such as "the cutting off of water supplies to trees, the overgrazing of the countryside, the unjustified killing of animals or feeding them harmful foods, the hunting of animals for sport, species extinction and the destruction of cultivated plant varieties, pollution of air and water, overconsumption of anything, and the waste of mineral and other resources" (Ehrenfield and Bentley n. d., p. 15; cited in Granberg-Michaelson 1984, p. 83). The community treated violators of *bal tashhit* like idolaters, excluding them from prayers and, virtually, from the community (Granberg-Michaelson 1984, p. 83).[13]

The king, therefore, had to maintain not only the just social political order of the state, but also the land's fertility. Should the king act justly he would achieve the "right and harmonious ordering of life in all its dimensions" (Rasmussen, 1987, pp. 120–21). If the king failed to bring prosperity to his people and country, he lost his dominion (Schmid 1973, p. 105; Foster 1981, pp. 24–25; Westermann 1982, p. 98; Rasmussen 1987, pp. 120–21).

Later, the scriptures "democratized" this understanding of righteous kingship, applying this understanding to all Jews. Material abundance then depended upon their collective, and individual, righteousness. Indeed, the story of King David, the one king who lived up to scriptural expectations, is as much a story about every person as it is a story about a particular king. After David, as ruler after ruler failed to follow his example, an intense longing developed for a ruler who would. Under such a ruler the people expected that the distortions in creation that arose due to lack of a proper ruler would vanish. Harmony and abundance would reign as in the beginning of creation (see Is 11:1–9) (Brueggemann 1968, p. 176; Moriarty 1968, p. 272; Baker 1979, p. 14).

Humanity and The Blessing

The king, and later the people, achieved this harmonious order by serving as a suitable conduit for the Creator's blessing that sustains all things. Westermann calls this "The Blessing," thereby distinguishing this fundamental activity of the Creator from other blessings. In Genesis 1, the Creator blesses the sea creatures saying, "Be fruitful and multiply and fill the waters in the seas, and let birds multiply on the earth" (vs. 22). Under the code of the priests of Israel, this blessing applied to all forms of life, human and nonhuman. The Creator continuously sustained all nations and creatures in a quiet way every day, providing the basis for creation's relation to its maker.

When the father, the head of the household, spoke the blessing over his family, the family received The Blessing. He served as the mediator between the Creator and the household. Later, the king and the priests also served as mediators of The Blessing. The welfare of the people and land depended upon the king and priests being political and religious sources of blessing. The king reflected the greatness and splendor of his people, a splendor resulting from The Blessing (Westermann 1982, pp. 78–112).[14]

Prior to the Hebrews entering the Promised Land, the Creator blessed the earth unconditionally. However, when the Hebrews were about to cross the Jordan River and enter the Promised Land, the Creator made The Blessing conditional—it depended upon Israel's obedience to him (Westermann 1982, p. 106).

> If you heed these ordinances, by diligently observing them, the Lord your God will maintain with you the covenant loyalty that he swore to your ancestors; he will love you, bless you, and multiply you; he will bless the fruit of your womb and the fruit of your ground, your grain and your wine and your oil, the increase of your cattle and the issue of your flock, in the land that he swore to your ancestors to give you. You shall be the most blessed of peoples, with neither sterility nor barrenness among you or your livestock. The Lord will turn away from you every illness. (Dt 7:12–15)

Therefore, all those who acted justly received The Blessing. This just behavior included generous giving to those in need. Because this abundant material blessing was almost always intended for the entire community, generous, wholehearted giving meant that no one would be left out. Its initial recipients acted as conduits of the Creator's provision. This spirit of giving protected the initial recipients of The Blessing from the temptation to hold onto the wealth for themselves, to rely on wealth instead of the goodness of the Creator for security. Generosity shielded the recipients from being hurt by abundance (Foster 1981, pp. 19–20).

Israel and, indeed, all nations mediated The Blessing to the land with which they lived in intimate, covenantal community.[15] The views on the relationship between humanity and its land in Genesis 1–11 apply to all nations, not just the Jews. The later passages that discuss Israel's relationship to creation thus are paradigmatic for all peoples (Clifford 1994, pp. 10–11). All peoples must care for their land and mirror the Creator's love for it.

The Jews considered the wilderness, the land where no one lived with the land, to be a scary place, the abode of wild beasts. The wild beasts did not need humans to mediate The Blessing. As Psalm 104 and other scriptures made clear, the wild animals received The Blessing directly from the Creator. These animals lived outside the covenant with Israel (although they lived within the covenant made with Noah). Humans cared for the land that they knew. They lived within the Garden, while other creatures lived in the wilderness (Pedersen 1991, pp. 479–84).[16]

Today humans affect almost every part of the globe directly or indirectly. The greenhouse effect, ozone holes, and garbage in oceans mean that even the most remote parts of the world feel our presence. We now garden the whole earth. While the ancient peoples bore no responsibility for the areas in which they did not live, for land with which they could have no relationship, there exists virtually no area where humans today have no impact. Consequently, we now are responsible to and for all of the earth because we now relate to all of it. It now increasingly depends upon our actions to determine whether or not it will prosper, whether or not it will receive The Blessing. The call to live justly with our land now extends to all the earth, our Garden, as does the call to "know" it, to live in relationship with it.[17]

We have seen that by the time of the Common Era, Judaism understood humans to be an integral part of creation. People lived with all other created things in total dependence upon the daily sustenance of the Creator who continually made and sustained the universe. People existed to serve creation and its creator by caring for the land upon which they depended and which, in turn, depended upon them. They lived in a garden that bore the imprint of those who cared for it. The very beings of the gardeners, in turn, bore the imprint of the land in which they lived. People and land together constituted a community living in covenant with the Creator.

Although part of creation, humans served as the Creator's viceregents within it. Because Judaism felt that the ideal king should serve the community of which he was a part, ideally humans reigned over the land as a shepherd caring for his flock, "laying down his life for his sheep." People served as the mediator of the Creator's blessing that sustained life, making the community of life fruitful and beautiful. When they lived compassionately and generously toward all, obedient to the Creator, all people and all creatures with which they had a relationship prospered. In doing so, people reflected the glory of the Creator—they individually became the Creator's image and corporately the Image.

Today, humans relate directly or indirectly with all parts of the globe. The question is whether or not humans will affect the world justly. If we wish to experience the depth of true humanity, we have to learn what it means to sacrifice for the sake of all of creation. We do not need necessarily to sacrifice our species for others, but at least we do need to relinquish some of the "essentials" of modern industrial life that all might prosper. We also need to reestablish our relationship with creation. This requires not just a romantic love affair with untrammeled nature, but a tested relationship between two partners who give and take. We need to know and respect the earth and to be known in return.

When we fail to do so and exploit creation, we fail to become fully human. As Bonifazi (1970) says, this does not require us to maintain creation in some pristine, unaltered state as if it were itself sacred. Nor does this allow us to change it at will every time it asserts its freedom and provokes us in some way. Rather, if we are to taste freedom as fully human people, we need to accord freedom to the rest of creation. Our covenant with creation demands that "we treat the world in such a way that our thinking about it and our handling of it release within us the power of becoming human, and elevate the status of things themselves through the treatment they receive" (pp. 229–30).

For most of us, life consists of bending our environment to suit our tastes, whether our environment be spouses, children, friends, field, or forest. It is risky to allow others to be who they are, because if we do, they might surprise us by doing something other than what we wanted. Yet, Jerusalem tells us that freedom and true joy comes from allowing others to be free, to give oneself freely to others in an intimate, life-giving relationship. Paradoxically, if we would live our lives fully, we must lose them by shedding old ways of seeing and acting and risking our very selves.

Notes

1. Similarly, no other word exists in ancient Hebrew for "nature" in the sense of a regulatory and creative physical power except for "God" (Robinson 1946, p. 1; cited in Dyrness 1987, p. 57).

2. Meeks (1989) points out that this Greek word for household refers to the site of production, distribution and consumption of the necessities of life—the site of human livelihood. It refers less to the family unit than the means of livelihood. In this book, where the family unit becomes all of creation, which itself is the means of livelihood, this distinction no longer applies.

3. Unless noted otherwise, all scriptural quotations are from the New Revised Standard Version of the Bible.

4. In describing the sea, Psalms 104:26 states, "There go the ships, and Leviathan that you formed to *sport* in it" (emphasis mine).

5. Schmid also points out that creation faith concerns the present world and humanity's natural environment, not so much the origin of the world.

6. "The essence of all pantheism, evolutionism, and modern cosmic religion is really in this proposition: that Nature is our mother. Unfortunately, if you regard nature as a mother, you discover that she is a stepmother. The main point of Christianity was this: that Nature is not our mother: Nature is our sister. We can be proud of her beauty, since we have the same father; but she has no authority over us; we have to admire, but not to imitate. This gives to the typically Christian pleasure in this earth a strange touch of lightness that is almost frivolity. . . . Nature is not solemn to Francis of Assisi or to George Herbert. To St. Francis, Nature is a sister, and even a younger sister: a little, dancing sister, to be laughed at as well as loved" (Chesterton 1909, p. 207).

7. This intimate relationship with an extrahuman creation that is alive is well illustrated by this quote from a Wintu Native American woman (thanks to Clyde Tilley who brought this quote to my attention): The White people never cared for land or deer or bear. When we Indians kill meat, we eat it all up. When we dig roots we make little holes. When we build houses, we make little holes. . . . We shake down acorns and pine nuts. We don't chop down trees. We only use dead wood. But White people plow up the ground, pull up the trees, kill everything. The trees say, "Don't, I am sore. Don't hurt me." But they chop it down and cut it up. The spirit of the land hates them. They blast out the trees and stir it up to its depths. They saw up the trees. They hurt them. The Indians never hurt anything, but the White people destroy all. They blast rocks and scatter them on the ground. The rock says "Don't. You are hurting me." But the White people pay no attention. When the Indians use rocks, they take little round ones for their cooking. . . . How can the spirit of the earth like the White man? Everywhere the White man has touched it, it is sore (Schilling 1974, p. 93).

8. Clifford (1988, p. 7) points out that Gn 2:4 though Gn 11 constitutes the entire second creation story. He also states that the newer creation story of Gn 1 actually represents more of an introduction to the second, an aid to its interpretation.

9. "God is love" (1Jn 4:16), that is, "being-with," leads by extension to the doctrine of the Trinity (Hall 1986, p. 120). The Christian tradition understands the Creator to be three persons so intensely relating to one another, so

interpenetrated, that they constitute one being. They refer, therefore, to "the Trinity" when they speak of God's communion-in-being, or three-personness. When humans live out community in its broadest, most loving form, they mirror the Creator, which itself is a community.

10. Page references for this source refer to pages in a photocopy of a final draft of the paper, not pages in the book.

11. While the Jews observed the Sabbath day and year, it appears that the jubilee remained an ideal seldom observed.

12. Of course, not only did the Jewish understanding of their creator influence their concept of kingship, but also their concept of kingship influenced their understanding of their creator. Thanks to Jim Dunkly for this point.

13. For more on the compassion embodied in the law toward the poor, animals, and land, see Foster (1981, pp. 28–30).

14. Westermann (1982, pp. 93, 110) points out that joy and beauty are the inevitable consequences of The Blessing.

15. The views on the relationship between humanity and its land in Genesis 1–11 apply to all nations, not just the Jews. The later passages that discuss Israel's relationship to creation thus are paradigmatic for all peoples (Clifford 1994, pp. 10–11). All peoples must care for their land and mirror the Creator's love for it.

16. This work was first published in 1926.

17. John Muir saw his mission in life as one of bringing urban people back into contact with creation. His society had lost touch with creation and he longed for people to know it personally as he did. For an intriguing study of Muir's relationship with creation and his role as a semiheretical Christian prophet see Austin (1987).

References

Austin, Richard Cartwright. 1987. *Baptized into Wilderness: A Christian Perspective on John Muir*. Atlanta: John Knox Press.

———. 1988. *Hope for the Land: Nature in the Bible*. Atlanta: John Knox Press.

Baker, John Austin. 1979. "Biblical Views of Nature." *Anticipation* 25 (January): 40–46.

Bonifazi, Conrad. 1970. "Biblical Roots of an Ecologic Conscience." Pp. 203–33 in *This Little Planet*, ed. Michael Hamilton. New York: Charles Scribner's Sons.

Brueggemann, Walter. 1968. "David and His Theologian." *Catholic Biblical Quarterly* 30(2): 156–81.

———. 1977. *The Land*. Philadelphia: Fortress Press.

———. 1983. *Interpretation: Genesis*. Atlanta: John Knox Press.

Chesterton, G. K. 1909. *Orthodoxy*. New York: John Lane Company.

Clifford, Richard J. 1988. "Creation in the Hebrew Bible." Pp. 151–70 in *Physics, Philosophy, and Theology: A Common Quest for Understanding*, ed. Robert J. Russell, William R. Stoeger, and G. V. Coyne. Vatican: Vatican Observatory.

———. 1994. "The Bible in the Environment." Pp. 1–26 in *Preserving the Creation: Environmental Theology and Ethics*, ed. Edmund Pellegrino, and Kevin Irwin. Washington, DC: Georgetown University Press.

Dyrness, William. 1987. "Stewardship of the Earth in the Old Testament." Pp. 50–65 in *Tending the Garden: Essays on the Gospel and the Earth*, ed. Wesley Granberg-Michaelson. Grand Rapids, MI: Eerdmans.

Ehrenfield, David, and Phillip J. Bentley. n.d. *Nature in the Jewish Tradition: The Source of Stewardship*. Unpublished manuscript.

Foster, Richard. 1981. *Freedom of Simplicity*. San Francisco: Harper and Row.

Granberg-Michaelson, Wesley. 1984. *A Worldly Spirituality: The Call to Redeem Life on Earth*. San Francisco: Harper & Row.

———. 1990. "Covenant and Creation." Pp. 27–36 in *Liberating Life: Contemporary Approaches to Ecological Theology*, ed. Charles Birch, William Eakin, and Jay B. McDaniel. Maryknoll, NY: Orbis.

Gregorios, Paolos Mar. 1987. "New Testament Foundations for Understanding the Creation." Pp. 83–92 in *Tending the Garden: Essays on the Gospel and the Earth*, ed. Wesley Granberg-Michaelson. Grand Rapids, MI: Eerdmans.

Hall, Douglas John. 1986. *Imaging God: Dominion as Stewardship*. Grand Rapids, MI: W. W. Eerdmans.

Koch, Klaus. 1983. "Is There a Doctrine of Retribution in the OT?" Pp. 57–87 in *Theodicy in the Old Testament*, ed. James L. Crenshaw. Philadelphia: Fortress Press.

Maly, Eugene H. 1968. "Genesis." Pp. 7–46 in *The Jerome Biblical Commentary*, ed. Raymond E. Brown, Joseph A. Fitzmyer, and Roland Murphy. Englewood Cliffs, NJ: Prentice-Hall.

Meeks, M. Douglas. 1989. *God the Economist: The Doctrine of God and Political Economy*. Minneapolis: Fortress Press.

Moriarty, Frederick L. 1968. "Isaiah 1–39." Pp. 265–82 in *The Jerome Biblical Commentary*, ed. Raymond E. Brown, Joseph A. Fitzmyer, and Roland E. Murphy. Englewood Cliffs, NJ: Prentice-Hall.

Pedersen, Johaness. 1991. *Israel. Its Life and Culture*. Atlanta: Scholars Press.

Rasmussen, Larry L. 1987. "Creation, Church, and Christian Responsibility." Pp. 114–31 in *Tending the Garden: Essays on the Gospel and the Earth*, ed. Wesley Granberg-Michaelson. Grand Rapids, MI: Eerdmans.

Schilling, S. Paul. 1974. *God Incognito*. Nashville: Abingdon Press.

Schmid, H. H. 1973. "Creation, Righteousness, and Salvation: Creation Theology as the Broad Horizon of Biblical Theology." Pp. 102–17 in *Creation in the Old Testament*, ed. Bernhard W. Anderson. Philadelphia: Fortress.

Tucker, Gene M. 1993. "Creation and the Limits of the World: Nature and History in the Old Testament." *Horizons in Biblical Theology* 15(2): 105–18.

Westermann, Claus. 1982. *Elements of Old Testament Theology*. Atlanta: John Knox Press.

Chapter 4

Saving Creation

Where there is no vision the people perish.—Proverbs 29:18 (King James)
Where there is no vision the people cast off restraint.—Proverbs 29:18
No people, society or organization can long exist without some compelling vision of the future that calls us forward into tomorrow.

—Kenneth Boulding

In chapter 3 we saw that generous self-giving leads to The Blessing that sustains creation. Communities of justice and compassion prosper. In this chapter we examine more carefully the ideal condition of creation, the attitude (interior state) necessary for achieving that condition, and the consequences of failing to do so. These considerations then lead us to consider how we can save creation from the degradation it suffers and what this implies for those concerned with improving human well-being.

The Significance of Grasping and Letting Go

The Hebrew scriptures describe the ideal condition of creation fully experiencing The Blessing as *shalom*. One author describes that state very well:

Its basic meaning is wholeness—a state of harmony among God, humanity and all creation. . . . All elements of creation are interrelated. Each

47

element participates in the whole creation, and if any element is denied wholeness and well-being (shalom), all are thereby diminished. This relational character of creation is rooted in all creatures' common origin in a God who not only created all that is but who continues to be active in the world, seeking our shalom. (Birch 1985, p. 1115; cited in Hall 1986, p. 118)

Shalom's wholeness embraces all things' well-being, which includes absence from fear, insecurity, oppression, hunger, disease—all the afflictions that rob creation of its joy and beauty. *Shalom* implies orderly fruitfulness and justice for all.

Achieving such a state requires that humanity, the species possessing the power to manage creation, do so with a spirit of generous caring. Humans driven by fear lack the ability to work wholeheartedly for the good of others. Those motivated by a "Theology of Enough," however, bring *shalom*, "a dancing kind of inter-relationship, seeking something more free than equality, more generous than equity, the ever-shifting equipoise of a life-system" (Willard 1974; cited in Foster 1981, p. 31).

Brueggemann states that the entire body of scriptures deals with the basic human tension between grasping and letting go, between accepting the blessings of the Creator as a gift over which we have no control, and grasping hold of them out of fear that they may cease to come. For instance, when the Hebrews first received the manna in the desert, the Creator warned them to gather only enough for that day's meals. However, those who gathered more to assure themselves of food for the next day found that the surplus rotted in their baskets. The Hebrews wandered forty years as a homeless people because they needed to learn how to depend upon the Creator, their shepherd, for their sustenance.

Before the Israelites crossed the Jordan into the Promised Land, according to the writers of Deuteronomy, the Creator made the rules of the game very clear:

When the Lord your God has brought you into the land that he swore to your ancestor . . . a land with fine, large cities that you did not build, houses filled with all sorts of goods that you did not fill, hewn cisterns that you did not hew, vineyards and olive groves that you did not plant—and when you have eaten your fill, take care that you do not forget the Lord, who brought you out of the land of Egypt, out of the house of slavery. (Dt 6:10–12)

Take care that you do not forget the Lord your God, by failing to keep his commandments, his ordinances, and his statutes, which I am commanding you today. When you have eaten your fill and have built fine houses and live in them . . . and all that you have is multiplied, then do not exalt yourself, forgetting the Lord your God . . . (who) led you through the great and terrible wilderness. . . . He made water flow for you from flint rock, and fed you in the wilderness with manna that your ancestors did not know, to humble you and to test you, and in the end to do you good. Do not say to yourself, "My power and the might of my own hand have gotten me this wealth." (Dt 8:11–17)

If you will only heed his every commandment that I am commanding you today—loving the Lord your God and serving him with all your heart and with all your soul—then he will give the rain for your land in its season, the early rain and the later rain, and you will gather in your grain, your wine, and your oil; and he will give grass in your fields for your livestock, and you will eat your fill. Take care, or you will be seduced into turning away, serving other gods and worshipping them, for then the anger of the Lord will be kindled against you and he will shut up the heavens, so that there will be no rain and the land will yield no fruit; then you will perish quickly off the good land that the Lord is giving you. (Dt 11:13–17)

Having entered and settled in the Promised Land, the Hebrews became accustomed to abundance and forgot the necessity of trusting in the source of that prosperity. Instead, they turned to the institution of kingship, political alliances, and oppression of the weak as ways of assuring control over the means of production, the land and its people, the apparent sources of future abundance. As a result, the Creator sent them into exile in Babylon where once more they had to learn the lesson that true freedom and prosperity only come from letting go of fear and trusting the Creator and one another.

The Hebrews' history of alternating between grasping and letting go reveals two models of *shalom*. For the landed living in abundance, their theology is one of The Blessing that leads to the *shalom* described above. Their challenge resides in remembering its source, managing resources wisely, and joyously caring for the land for the sake of future generations. For the landless, their theology is one of salvation, of being saved from life-threatening circumstances and of having *shalom* restored. Those living precariously as exiles and homeless people cry out to their Creator who hears their cry, overcomes the chaos and disorderliness threatening creation, and restores *shalom* to the land. In either case, The Blessing or deliverance comes when the people live in right relationship with their creator (Brueggemann 1976, pp. 28–36; Westermann 1982, p. 113).

In order to help the Hebrews remember to let go, to trust, the Creator established the Sabbath. Every seventh day the Hebrews refrained from work of any kind. Even the slaves, fields, and animals rested on that day. The Creator rested on the seventh day, demonstrating that the Maker of all things did not have to wrestle continuously against the chaos in the universe. The Creator remained firmly in control at all times. Similarly, the Creator's people rested on the seventh day as a way of remembering who is in control. The Sabbath reminded them that their feverish attempts to secure their livelihood ultimately did not bring them security. Rather, their security rested in the One who sustained them. Observing the Sabbath taught them to let go, to cease grasping for control and power.

The Sabbath laws also maintained the outward expression of justice, as well as cultivating its inner prerequisite (Austin 1987, pp. 104–8). Every forty-nine years, during the Jubilee year, owners had to free their Hebrew slaves and forgive fellow countrymen their debts. The land, too, had its own rights and duties. It rested, not only every seventh day but, especially, every seventh year:

> in the seventh year there shall be a Sabbath of complete rest for the land, a Sabbath for the Lord: you shall not sow your field or prune your vineyard. You shall not reap the aftergrowth of your harvest or gather the grapes of your unpruned vine. (Lev 25:4, 5)

> the seventh year you shall let it rest and lie fallow, so that the poor of your people may eat; and what they leave the wild animals may eat. (Ex 23:11)

When the Hebrews failed to keep these Sabbaths for the land, grasping for more harvests and wealth, the Levitical priests prophesied:

> you I will scatter among the nations, and I will unsheathe the sword against you: your land shall be a desolation, and your cities a waste. Then the land shall enjoy its Sabbath years as long as it lies desolate, while you are in the land of your enemies; then the land shall rest, and enjoy its Sabbath years. As long as it lies desolate, it shall have the rest it did not have on your Sabbaths when you were living on it. (Lv 26: 34, 35)

The people of the ancient Near East, including the Hebrews, believed that, while creation represented a powerful act of the gods/Creator against chaos and formlessness, this disorder continually threatened creation's harmonious order. Chaos took many forms: famine, disease, mental illness, marital and generational estrangement, trickery and corruption, oppression, denial of goods to the poor and weak, exile, and poverty (Rasmussen 1987, p. 120). When people failed to care slavishly for the Garden and focused on themselves, they worked their own destruction by failing to fulfill their vocation as human beings (Brueggemann 1983, p. 48).

When individuals, and a people, acted contrary to the demands of justice, chaos intruded. When humans acted outside of a loving relationship with their covenant partners (the Creator, other humans, and the land), they deprived their community of the ongoing blessing that keeps chaos at bay. These actions broke the covenant relationship that maintains order. The Jews originally thought such actions came back relatively quickly upon the individual who performed them, so that individuals bore the consequences of their own actions, whether good or bad. Not only that, the land and its inhabitants prospered or suffered accordingly. Later, the Jews and early Christians came to see that the consequences of an individual's actions might only rebound on the individual at a later time, even after life. In any case, individuals created their own world and their own inevitable punishment. The world that resulted from such actions fell far short of that intended by the Creator. By failing to act within the established order, unjust people inevitably set in motion the destruction of creation.

The Deluge represents the first incident of environmental degradation. The authors of Genesis relate that prior to the Deluge people lived in an ever-increasing spiral of violence and grasping for power. The flood represented the inevitable consequence of their actions. The world could start over again only after enduring the waters that cleansed the world of injustice. The writers use the same word for the destruction of the world as for the destruction that the people already had wreaked upon the world. The Creator merely ratifies what they wrought (Clifford 1988, p. 165). The story warns us that very powerful mechanisms exist to bring the world back to unity and order (Brueggemann 1983, p. 75).

The law and the prophets elaborate extensively on this connection. For instance, after the prophet Hosea catalogs the great injustice and evil in Israel, he proclaims:

> Therefore the land mourns, and all who live in it languish;
> together with the wild animals
> and the birds of the air,
> even the fish of the sea are perishing. (4:3)

In the book of Leviticus, the Creator, speaking through Moses, warns the Hebrews about the wickedness of the people who lived in the Promised Land before them:

Do not defile yourselves in any of these ways, for by all these practices the nations I am casting out before you have defiled themselves. Thus the land became defiled; and I punished it for its iniquity, and the land vomited out its inhabitants. But you shall keep my statutes and my ordinances and commit none of these abominations . . . otherwise the land will vomit you out for defiling it, as it vomited out the nation that was before you. (18:24–28)

Finally, through Zephaniah the Creator went so far as to warn the people that their actions actually *unmake* creation:

I will utterly sweep away everything from the face of the earth, says the Lord.
I will sweep away humans and animals;
I will sweep away the birds of the air and the fish of the sea.
I will make the wicked stumble.
I will cut off humanity from the face of the earth, says the Lord. (1:2, 3)

Note that first humans perish, followed by animals, birds, and fish—exactly the opposite of the order of creation in Genesis (Dyrness 1987, p. 61). The prophet warns his people that the survival of creation in the face of chaos depends upon their wholehearted commitment to their covenant partners, upon their obedience, compassion, and mercy.

According to Jewish thought, then, the very stability of the world depends upon human actions. If we embody justice in our relationships with one another and all of creation, living in obedience to the Creator, then creation remains intact. The Blessing that sustains the world order flows through humans to the world they create. However, if we fail to live this way, we not only degrade ourselves but destroy the world by our actions. Our individual interior state and, ultimately, the justice of our society determine the fate of creation.

Wisdom as Letting Go

We have seen that letting go of control leads to *shalom* whereas grasping leads to chaos. The Jews also realized that knowledge plays a role in prosperity. They linked letting go and knowledge intimately together.

According to Jewish thought, humans receive the commission to work as part of the commandment to care for and cultivate the Garden. The Blessing, therefore, accompanies work. Successful cultivation, however, requires understanding how the Garden functions, the order of creation as intended by the Creator.

Intellectual activity, reflection, and contemplation of how to improve one's living space, obtain food, perform daily tasks, and live with others all belong to what the Hebrews called "wisdom." Wisdom meant knowing how to steer one's way through life. By failing in an attempt to build a house or to make good friends, we learn because we reflect on that failure, gain insights, and eventually realize success. Wisdom, therefore, was thoroughly pragmatic, oriented to what demonstrably worked (Westermann 1982, pp. 98–100; Johnston 1987).[1]

Proverbs 8 declares that the Creator implanted wisdom, personified as a woman, to bring life to the world.

> I love those who love me,
>   and those who seek me
>   diligently find me.
> Riches and honor are with me,
>   enduring wealth and prosperity . . .
> (W)hen he marked out
>   the foundations of the earth,
>   then I was beside him, like a
>   master worker;
> and I was daily his delight,
>   rejoicing before him always,
> rejoicing in his inhabited world
>   and delighting in the
>   human race . . .
> Happy is the one who listens to
>   me,
>   watching daily at my gates,
>   waiting beside my doors.
> For whoever finds me finds life
>   and obtains favor from the
>   Lord;
> but those who miss me injure
>   themselves;
>   all who hate me love death. (vs. 17–18, 29–31, 34–36)

Wisdom lives in the world offering humans intimacy, knowledge of the Creator, and prosperity. Reflective work, therefore, brings about The Blessing.

The realization that the Creator reigns supreme over all removes the supernatural from creation. While creation delights its maker, it possesses no supernatural powers. This understanding frees humans to deal rationally with creation, to understand and manage it subject to the knowledge that they cannot use it as they wish. Rather, they care for it as loyal servants of both Creator and creation, which exists largely because the Creator desires it for its own sake.

Wisdom, therefore, avoids all attempts to force creation to fit human needs, because creation has its own rights before the Creator. Rather, humans must take the Garden as a given, learning how to work with it and trusting that thereby they will enter *shalom*, the land of milk and honey. If the Creator made the world a certain way, they must assume that it did so for a purpose. Loyalty to the Creator requires the Creator's representatives to respect that purpose, even if they do not understand it (Baker 1979, pp. 19–21).

Wisdom, then, requires letting go of the way we want things to be, of desiring to be in charge and to control, and learning to cooperate with the natural rhythms of life. The Garden becomes the arena within which we learn how to let go and to die to our self-centeredness. In turn, it becomes the place where we learn how to live fully and to become fully human, by giving wholeheartedly to others and trusting in a benevolent creator. The Blessing, accordingly, depends upon our interior state and our knowledge of how the world works, which are both aspects of wisdom.

Intimacy in the Cosmos

The early Christians built upon these concepts in an interesting way. At the time of Christ, certain circles within Judaism despaired because the Promised Land lay under Roman occupation and the world seemed beyond redemption. They longed for the Creator to start over, to establish a new order that would banish evil. The writers of the New Testament responded to this despair by claiming that people could be delivered from this helplessness. By allowing themselves to be transformed by the Creator, they, in turn, could transform the cosmos that waits to be reborn:

> The creation waits with eager longing for the revealing of the children of God . . . in hope that the creation itself will be set free from its bondage to decay and will obtain the freedom of the glory of the children of God. We know that the whole creation has been groaning in labor pains until now;

and not only the creation, but we ourselves . . . groan inwardly while we wait for . . . the redemption of our bodies. (Rom 8:19–23)

Liberating people from helplessness became the prerequisite for the entire remaking of the cosmos in the Creator's time (Baker 1979, pp. 22–24). They saw Jesus as the Creator's answer to a suffering creation. The early Christians understood Jesus as the "Image of God," the Creator who became human. They believed that the Creator loved creation intensely, and passionately desired to overcome the tendency of humanity to turn away from the Creator, taking all of creation along with it. So, the Creator of all things became part of the created order by becoming a member of the species that governed creation. Becoming a human being, somehow bringing together the Creator and the created, the Creator restored the unity and dialogue with creation that had started in the Garden. The early Christians reasoned that, when all people chose to enter into a close relationship with Jesus, all of creation, not just humans, would be restored to intimacy with the Creator. Restoring the vice-regents of creation to a right relationship with the Creator would allow The Blessing to flow freely to creation.[2]

The poetry of the early church expressed a concept that offered even more hope—the Cosmic Christ. Jesus became identified with the logos, the eternal Word spoken by the Creator in continually making the world, as well as wisdom.

In the beginning was the Word, and the Word was with God, and the Word was God. He was in the beginning with God. All things came into being through him, and without him not one thing came into being. (Jn 1:1–3; see also Heb 1–2)

He is the image of the invisible God, the firstborn of all creation; for in him all things in heaven and on earth were created, things visible and invisible, whether thrones or dominions or rulers or powers—all things have been created through him and for him. He himself is before all things, and in him all things hold together. . . . For in him all the fullness of God was pleased to dwell, and through him God was pleased to reconcile to himself all things, whether on earth or in heaven, by making peace through the blood of his cross. (Col 1:15–20)

The Word sustains and creates all things. Just as all people live "in" the world they have created by their word/actions, so now all live "in" the Word.[3] By living "in" the Word, being united in the One who permeates all matter, all creatures live united to one another and the Creator, with Jesus as the head of creation (Metzger 1991). In this sense, creation has become the body of the Creator, the Word. By becoming creation and voluntarily submitting to execution (to destruction), the Word took upon itself all the inevitable consequences of human actions leading to the destruction of creation. In this way it saves creation, making *shalom* possible once more.[4]

While the great rebirth of creation described by Paul occurred with the incarnation of the Word, the transformation's maturation depends upon humans aligning themselves with the Word, thereby reuniting themselves with the rest of creation and the Creator. Humans now have the task of reconciling all of the cosmos to the Creator by becoming reconciled to the Creator first themselves (2 Cor 5:18–20).[5]

All of creation now teems with the life of the Creator in a special way. Accordingly, people can come to know the Creator by knowing creation—both by understanding it and by developing a personal relationship with it that permits one to "see" what is there.

The latter resembles the predicament of the fish who wanted to learn about water. The sages of his species had told him that water coursed through them and enveloped them. It supported his body and his very existence. All food and communication came to him via the very thing he could not see. In fact, they said, water formed most of his body. But, he could not see it. He swam frustratedly from sage to sage in his search for someone who could open his eyes. One day he gave up. As he floated, still among the currents, he started noticing hints of movement as the water flowed over his skin. When he moved his fins, he felt a slight resistance and pressure. Having slowed down, he noticed the world in which he lived and came to know the basis of his existence.

In the same way, Christianity prior to the Enlightenment, and the Orthodox and Roman Catholic traditions in particular today, sees creation as infused with the presence of the Creator. As St. Maximus said, "The world is a diaphany through which Jesus Christ is shining." For this reason everything becomes sacred to those who "see" the One who is in all things (Maloney 1979, pp. 35–36). All creation has value now, not only because it delights the Creator, but because creation resides in the Creator. The Word, the matrix of creation, intimately involves itself with all of creation.

The Word, then, transforms the cosmos, and continues to transform it, in three basic ways. First, by the Word's becoming part of the created order, the creation, both visible and invisible, now forms the Word's body. Second, by becoming human, the Word closely identifies with all humans, the heads of creation. All have access to it. Third, those who have close communion with it by actively following it incorporate themselves in it in an especially intimate way, so that as a group they reflect its presence actively to the world (Gregorios 1987, pp. 88–91).[6] The Creator now "rules over the world by assuming it" (Bonifazi 1970, p. 226).

The injunction to "love your neighbor as yourself" now takes on new meaning. All creation, present and future, warrants humanity's loving care and compassion as described in the parable of the Good Samaritan and in the Sermon on the Mount (Mt 5–7; Lk 6:17–46). As Niebuhr said:

Who, finally, is my neighbor, the companion whom I have been commanded to love as myself? [The neighbor] is the near one and the far one; the one removed from me by distances in time and space, in convictions and loyalties. . . . The neighbor is in past and present and future, yet [the neighbor] is not simply [humankind] in its totality but rather in its articulation, the community of individuals in community. [The neighbor] is Augustine in the Roman Catholic Church and Socrates in Athens, and the Russian people, and the unborn generations who will bear the consequences of our failures, future persons for whom we are administering the entrusted wealth of nature and other greater common gifts. [The neighbor] is [humanity] and [the neighbor] is angel and [the neighbor] is animal and inorganic being, all that participates in being. (Niebuhr 1956, p. 38)[7]

Salvation, Proclamation, and the Coming *Shalom*

If we are to save creation as we know it from the degradation we see all about us, we must start within.

The natural world is an actor in biblical history and not merely through the agency of humankind, the "head" of the natural creation. Nature plays a role in the history of salvation or better engages in and is transformed by the epic events. So I can speak legitimately of the redemption of nature. . . . The human spirit corrupts nature, and man is one with nature. Humankind belongs wholly to the realm of nature, mortal. His attempt to become a god, to transcend the insecurity of mortal flesh, is his primal sin. He is not half-god, half-animal. His soul contains no spark of the divine. He is an animal, a stately animal, theomorphic indeed, but he cannot free himself now or in the Beyond from nature. In him nature is an actor in the drama of salvation, and also apart from him nature is an actor, fleeing the divine wrath, transfigured by the divine glory, redeemed insofar as man is redeemed, damned insofar as humanity is damned. (Cross 1989, pp. 95–96)

> If my people who are called by my name humble themselves, pray, seek
> my face, and turn from their wicked ways, then I will hear from heaven,
> and will forgive their sin and heal their land. (2 Chr 7:14)

If grasping has led to all these troubles, surely the answer to environmental degradation lies in letting go. The *sine qua non* for saving creation consists of humanity's letting go of its desire to control creation
(self, others, and "nature"). Humans have to do this because, as the
great prophet Pogo once said, "We have met the enemy and he is us."

When deciding whether or not to destroy the world the first time, the
authors of Genesis describe the Creator as being grieved by what was
happening on earth. At the instigation of the Creator, the only humans
left who still lived in communion with their Creator saved creation from
the Deluge. Help came from within creation itself. In order to bring
relief to the world, the Word later entered into the world and took on its
pain so that rebirth could occur. As Isaiah the prophet said, "he was
wounded for our transgressions, crushed for our iniquities; upon him
was the punishment that made us whole, and by his bruises we are
healed" (Is 53:5). Noah prefigured the help that came to creation later
when the Word became creation in order to save it a second time.

If we, the vice-regents of creation, wish to heal the earth, we, too,
must enter into the suffering of the earth. We must let go of the security
of insularity, of believing that somehow our actions have no moral consequence on others. Instead, we must have compassion toward creation
and suffer with it. Part of accepting this suffering implies acknowledging what we have done and asking forgiveness from both the Creator
and creation. In a family, when one member hurts another, only the
asking and granting of forgiveness can restore harmony to the community. Similarly, in creation only asking and granting forgiveness can
restore wholeness. Because the essence of being human is "being-
with," we become truly human and truly healers only by living with all
of creation in its suffering, seeking reconciliation with it and seeking to
end its anguish.

The next step then consists of letting go of the illusion that we as
individuals and as a species control creation. The Jews see creation
somewhat as an orchestra. An orchestra whose members play whatever
piece they wish at any time, regardless of the will of the director, produces cacophony, even to the most modern of ears. This occurs because
the players disregard their relationship to the conductor and to one another. However, letting go of their desires to follow their own whims,
reestablishing their relationship with the conductor, and listening to

those around them unleashes incredible power and beauty capable of transforming both players and audience.

In the Garden, the spirit of the Creator acts as the conductor of the orchestra of creation. When humans open themselves to a relationship with the spirit, listen to it, and follow its directions, all work together to create something unseen and unheard before. Creation cannot help being affected by the result.

The Jewish prophets anticipated that such a radical reordering of relationships would transform creation and bring *shalom*. Isaiah 35 gives a good example of what they expected. The chapter begins with the heavenly herald proclaiming that the Creator has come to save Zion from exile and that both Zion and creation should take hope. As a result, the desert will bloom and rejoice, and the glory of the Creator will fill the land. The blind will see, the deaf hear, and the lame leap for joy. In Isaiah 35 and 65, a redeemed humanity lives in a healed world where peace, health, and joy—*shalom*—reign. The integrated mind, body, and spirit of all beings will be restored to wholeness.

In keeping with this understanding, Jesus announced the beginning of his earthly ministry by quoting Isaiah 61:1–2, proclaiming healing and liberation, a year of favor from the Creator. His last words to his disciples in the gospel of Mark carry the same message: "Go into all the world and proclaim the good news to the whole creation" (16:15). Proclaiming means shouting as a herald to creation, as in Isaiah 35. Truly proclaiming healing to creation implies that we will have radically reoriented our vision of the world from one of humanity isolated from itself and "nature" to humanity living in intimate, covenantal love with the Garden. This vision of the Garden impels us to relate in new ways to the rest of creation. As a result of our effective, lived-out proclamation, creation experiences a new humanity that treads lightly upon the earth, bringing healing and wholeness, peace and prosperity to all. Creation experiences the change and thereby knows the "revelation of the children of God."

Conclusions and Lessons for Socioecological Thought

We have seen that grasping for control brings about the destruction of the cosmos whereas letting go and trusting the Creator and the created order brings *shalom*. Achieving shalom requires that humanity open its ears fully to the voice of the Creator and follow the Creator's guidance, bringing into maturity the intimacy between the Creator and creation established when the image of the Creator became human. Transformed human beings image the Image, making it present and operative in the world. Accordingly, they possess the power to proclaim healing effectively to the cosmos, to bring about the Garden once more.

This healing translates itself into everyday human activities when humans first observe creation to discern how the composer has orchestrated the score of life. By following the score and the conductor, humanity's day-to-day activities bring wholeness and life to all. Observing and listening to creation brings humans into touch with the deep reality undergirding all things. This reinforces their respect for creation and the desire to cooperate with it.

This worldview holds many lessons for modern humanity, and particularly for those concerned with human welfare and ending environmental degradation. Whether or not one adheres to the tenets of Judaism or Christianity, basic aspects of the Jewish-Christian worldview have much to say to us as we enter the twenty-first century.

The West, and particularly U.S.-British tradition, regards individual well-being as almost sacred. Policies rise and fall on the basis of their impact on the individual. However, the view of the Garden warns the West that the individual does not live in splendid isolation. Rather, in some way individuals are designed to live intimately with all things. When they do not, someone or something suffers. To the extent that some part of creation suffers, all suffer.

We share createdness with all things. As created beings we all live subject to a much greater force that creates us and sustains our very being. Because all things live in this force and all things respond to it, we live in community with all creation and that which sustains it. Because the creative force in all things delights in creation, we must respect all things and their right to prosper. Doing so is tantamount to respecting oneself. We exist to care for creation and to see that it prospers. When we fail to seek the good of all creation, human and otherwise, we fail in our vocation. Therefore, we are responsible to creation and the creative force for the way we live.

Ultimately, we are gardeners. The Garden shapes and nourishes us, just as we shape and care for the Garden. Without the Garden we starve—and we lose our meaning. Without us, the Garden loses its spokesperson and the creative force, its conversation with creation.

All of this carries implications for human well-being. As noted above, the Jews viewed humans as possessing physical, mental, and spiritual capacities that could not be separated from one another. Full human development, or maximum human well-being, then, requires progress in three related areas: meeting one's basic physical and social needs, development of one's mental capacity, and spiritual growth. The latter two areas include developing creative and interpersonal abilities, a sense of solidarity with others, unselfishness and self-giving for the sake of others, and communion with the Creator.[8]

The early Christian thought that emerged from this worldview saw that accepting more than the basic amount of goods fosters human growth only when it leads to mental or spiritual growth. An unending succession of increasing material wealth typically endangers human well-being because accumulation tends to displace concern for others and the Creator and to become paramount in one's life. Materialism causes the creature, whose essence is "being-with" others, to focus on itself, not others. Driving for more than "just enough" too easily causes humans to fail to image the Creator and to fail to achieve the purpose for which they were made. Materialism, therefore, represents a state of human underdevelopment rather than a driving force for true development. Another form of grasping, materialism leads people to seek well-being in goods rather than in the source of all life. It also leads people to attempt to control the means of producing goods, other humans, and extrahuman creation, in order to assure themselves of future goods.

Materialism and overconsumption represent a threat to our well-being as surely as does grinding poverty. Reducing creation to a source of utility, a source of raw materials, and a means to the end of satisfying our insatiable desires, therefore, represents grasping for control and exploiting those with whom we are in community (Brueggemann 1976, p. 194). It also means that we elevate material goods to the prime goal of our life, endangering our well-being as human beings. The exploitation to which materialism leads degrades humans, making them less than human and depriving them of the joy that is the hallmark of *shalom*. Achieving or maintaining *shalom*, therefore, represents a special challenge and task for those who control the means of production: the affluent of society. It also represents a special task for the species that bears the authority in the world to make decisions and alter its makeup: humanity.

Our desire to control creation to serve human ends leads us to attempt to change nature in our image, rather than to image healing to creation. Exploiting and bending creation to make it behave as we wish constitutes overweening pride on our part, a pride that brings not only environmental degradation but many other ills as well. The attitude that allows us to objectify and thereby remove the personal element from creation allows us to do the same to anything else—minorities, women, children, the unborn, future generations, species, ecosystems, and entire landscapes. Poverty, war, discrimination, pollution, oppression, and extinction of species and the unborn all stem from our desire to control rather than cooperate. Self-serving individualism, grasping after prosperity out of fear of losing what we have or of not getting it in the future, leads to personal, communal, and environmental destruction. Thus, dealing with the root cause of suffering in any form leads to healing on many fronts. Improving human well-being requires letting go of extreme individualism and learning generosity and openness to the Other in humans and all of creation.[9]

Just as we must care for creation now, willingly limiting our insatiable desires or reforming unjust societies so that adequate living conditions permit all creation to prosper, we must care for creation for future generations.[10] Caring for creation is a multigenerational responsibility. Just as King Hezekiah in Isaiah 39:5–7 was rebuked for attempting to secure his generation's well-being at the expense of future generation's security, so will we if we attempt to do the same (Brueggemann 1976, p. 194).

We cannot isolate spiritual, political, economic, and ecological systems from one another. They are linked together by one reality, greatly affected by the way humans think and, therefore, act. If we wish to heal the world, we must start with ourselves by reassessing the way we see the world and the values that actually guide our behavior. Environmental justice requires justice for all, a justice that starts within each one of us. Saving "the environment" ultimately leads us to confront the most daunting challenge of all—saving ourselves from ourselves.

So far we have examined how humans are supposed to relate to the Garden. We learned that wise gardeners come to understand what works and does not work by observing the results of their actions and availing themselves of others' insights. They play a key part in one large, complex system. So far, however, we have not considered how the Garden functions as an integrated socio-biophysical system. To avoid flunking Gardening 101, therefore, we need wisdom. Accordingly, the next chapters examine the interactions of the biophysical and human systems in terms of economic growth, attitudes, and institutions.

Notes

1. Although some debate exists as to exactly what constitutes the body of wisdom literature in the Hebrew scriptures, the following probably can be in-

cluded: Proverbs, Ecclesiastes, Job, some Psalms, the Song of Songs, Ecclesiasticus, and the Wisdom of Solomon (Johnston 1987, pp. 67–68).

2. The relationship of human to Creator now includes both differentiation and identification. Just as the Trinity involves three distinct persons intensely "being-with" each other, so does the relationship of person to Creator now involve intense "being-with" one another. This precludes the total loss of the individual as in pantheism and Neoplatonism but allows for deep intimacy (Hall 1986, pp. 120–21).

3. See Koch (1983) for a discussion of being "in" one's actions. The Hebrew scriptures felt that one created a powerful sphere of influence about oneself as the result of one's actions.

4. Although the Word is identified with Jesus, I use the pronoun "it" to refer to the Word.

5. O'Rourke (1968, p. 281) points out that the word for world in 2 Cor 5:19 is *kosmos*, which refers primarily to humanity, but humanity in the sense of the impact its grasping has had on the rest of creation.

6. Within the Hebrew and New Testament scriptures a tension exists concerning the nature of the world in the future. Some scriptures talk about the destruction of the old and the creation of a "new heaven and a new earth." Others talk about the restoration of the original state of harmony in the Garden. Discussion of this controversy takes us on to a tangent. However, good discussions of these views can be found in Zerbe (1992) and Baker (1979). However, as Zerbe points out, the problem ultimately lies not with creation but with humanity's insistence on grasping for power, as symbolized in Adam and Eve's grasping for knowledge by taking the apple in Eden. The scriptures are clear on how humans should relate to all of creation. What form creation will take in the future ultimately makes no difference in how we behave to it now. Zerbe, indeed, maintains that the images of the world "passing away" refer more to refinement and purification of the world to rid the earth of evil, rather than to destroy and replace it.

For a thought-provoking discussion of the meaning of Jesus and the social reality of the kingdom as reflected in land, see Brueggemann (1977, pp. 170–73).

7. Following Rasmussen (1987, p. 118), the original source of this quote, "he" and "man" have been replaced by "neighbor" and "humanity."

8. With respect to the importance of the social dimension, Boulding (1966) makes a similar point when he asserts that the welfare of the individual depends on the extent to which he or she identifies him- or herself with others.

9. Of course, science and materialism have led to technological advances as well as increases in living standards for a significant proportion of the human populace. However, I argue that they have come at great cost. As I argue later, different values lead to different science, technology, motivations, and institutions. I do not wish to argue for returning to some romantic state of nature. Rather, I argue that our vision of who we and our world are inevitably shapes

our actions in ways that bring about greater or less wholeness. We have achieved remarkable advances on many fronts and lost on many others. It is time to seek balance and integratedness.

10. Chapters 5 and 6 discuss how human institutions and poverty bring about environmental degradation.

References

Austin, Richard Cartwright. 1987. "Rights for Life: Rebuilding Human Relationships with the Land." Pp. 102–26 in *Theology of the Land*, eds. Bernard F. Evans, and Gregory D. Cusack. Collegeville, Minn.: The Liturgical Press.

Baker, John Austin. 1979. "Biblical Views of Nature." *Anticipation* 25 (January): 40–46.

Birch, Bruce C. 1985. "Old Testament Foundations for Peacemaking in a Nuclear Age." *The Christian Century* 102(38): 1115.

Bonifazi, Conrad. 1970. "Biblical Roots of an Ecologic Conscience." Pp. 203–33 in *This Little Planet*, ed. Michael Hamilton. New York: Charles Scribner's Sons.

Boulding, Kenneth E. 1966. "The Economics of the Coming Spaceship Earth." Ch. 1 in *Environmental Quality in a Growing Economy*, ed. H. Jarrett. Baltimore: Johns Hopkins University Press.

Brueggemann, Walter. 1976. *Living Toward a Vision: Biblical Reflections on Shalom*. Philadelphia: United Church Press.

———. 1977. *The Land*. Philadelphia: Fortress Press.

———. 1983. *Interpretation: Genesis*. Atlanta: John Knox Press.

Clifford, Richard J. 1988. "Creation in the Hebrew Bible." Pp. 151-70 in *Physics, Philosophy, and Theology: A Common Quest for Understanding*, eds. Robert J. Russell, William R. Stoeger, and G. V. Coyne. Vatican: Vatican Observatory.

Cross, Frank Moore. 1989. "The Redemption of Nature." *Princeton Seminary Bulletin* 10(2): 94–104.

Dyrness, William. 1987. "Stewardship of the Earth in the Old Testament." Pp. 50–65 in *Tending the Garden: Essays on the Gospel and the Earth*, ed. Wesley Granberg-Michaelson. Grand Rapids, Mich.: Eerdmans.

Foster, Richard. 1981. *Freedom of Simplicity*. San Francisco: Harper and Row.

Gregorios, Paolos Mar. 1987. "New Testament Foundations for Understanding the Creation." Pp. 83-92 in *Tending the Garden: Essays on the Gospel and the Earth*, ed. Wesley Granberg-Michaelson. Grand Rapids, Mich.: Eerdmans.

Hall, Douglas John. 1986. *Imaging God: Dominion as Stewardship*. Grand Rapids, Mich.: Eerdmans.

Johnston, Robert K. 1987. "Wisdom Literature and its Contribution to a Biblical Environmental Ethic." Pp. 66–82 in *Tending the Garden: Essays on the*

Gospel and the Earth, ed. Wesley Granberg-Michaelson. Grand Rapids, Mich.: Eerdmans.

Koch, Klaus. 1983. "Is There a Doctrine of Retribution in the OT?" Pp. 57–87 in *Theodicy in the Old Testament*, ed. James L. Crenshaw. Philadelphia: Fortress Press.

Maloney, George, A. 1979. *Invaded by God: Mysticism and the Indwelling Trinity*. Denville, NJ: Dimension Books.

Metzger, Bruce M. 1991. "Introduction to the Letter of Paul to the Ephesians." P. 272 in *The New Oxford Annotated Bible*, eds. Bruce M. Metzger, and Roland E. Murphy. New York: Oxford University Press.

Niebuhr, H. Richard. 1956. *The Purpose of the Church and Its Ministry: Reflections on the Aims of Theological Education*. New York: Harper and Row.

O'Rourke, John J. 1968. "The Second Letter to the Corinthians." Pp. 276–90 in *The Jerome Biblical Commentary*, eds. Raymond E. Brown, Joseph A. Fitzmyer, and Roland E. Murphy. Englewood Cliffs, NJ: Prentice-Hall.

Rasmussen, Larry L. 1987. "Creation, Church, and Christian Responsibility." Pp. 114–31 in *Tending the Garden: Essays on the Gospel and the Earth*, ed. Wesley Granberg-Michaelson. Grand Rapids, Mich.: Eerdmans.

Westermann, Claus. 1982. *Elements of Old Testament Theology*. Atlanta: John Knox Press.

Willard, Dallas. 1974. "Lecture on the Sermon on the Mount." Woodlake Avenue Friends Church, Canoga, Calif. Unpublished.

Zerbe, Gordon. 1992. "Ecology According to the New Testament." *Direction* 21(2): 15–26.

Chapter 5

Tilling the Garden: Creation and the Economy

So far we have seen that the Judeo-Christian tradition that serves as the foundation for much of Western culture views humans as part of the created order, not as something separate from it. The Creator put people into the created order to care for it on the Creator's behalf, as well as to draw sustenance from it. As a result of the covenant between the Creator, humans, and the land, human well-being depends upon cooperating with the natural processes of the Garden, giving from the heart to others, and maintaining an obedient relationship with the Other. Relationships play the key role in maintaining the health of the Garden.

Similarly, we have seen that relationships play a key role in the analysis of the processes of the Garden. Individual components of this system interact with the other components to codetermine one another. These interactions produce a mix of goods and services in such a way that the production of one of these depends upon the amount being produced of the others. Moreover, landscapes exhibit economies of configuration. The mix of the goods and services produced by a natural system depends upon the spatial relationship of the natural systems in a landscape. Finally, processes at the supraglobal scale appear to link the well-being of all of creation to humanity's justice. The spiritual and material link up in ways we only barely can imagine.

In chapter 2 we asked three questions: (1) Can humans dominate the rest of creation with impunity? (2) Should we attempt to dominate it, or rather should we attempt to cooperate with nonhuman creation and its processes? (3) Can we fully understand the mechanisms that affect our answer, or do we confront problems of scale? Having laid both the ecological and moral frameworks for answering these questions, we now can analyze the economic, historical, political, and cultural processes that affect all of creation's well-being.

Amidst all this discussion of relationships, we have discussed economic relationships very little, which might seem odd for a book written by an economist. Let me explain why.

Any discipline, whether economics, English, or history, rests upon a view of the world that tells it how the world functions, what questions to ask, and how one obtains knowledge. Modern neoclassical economics, the mainstream school of thought within the discipline, rests on the British utilitarianism of eighteenth- and nineteenth-century thinkers such as Jeremy Bentham and John Stuart Mill. Schools of economics that take different beginning points from that of the neoclassical school ask other questions, analyze in different ways, and generally see the world quite differently. Given the environmental issues facing us at the end of the twentieth century, and the likelihood that we will be living with them for a long time to come, we might well ask whether London's worldview suffices in answering our questions or whether Jerusalem's might do better. Having developed the worldview of the Garden, we can proceed to build a land economics based on that foundation and compare it to the traditional version.

In beginning to address our questions from an economic perspective, we first must establish the fact that any growth implies change, and that economic activity implies changing natural systems. We then will examine how the inevitable altering of natural systems can contribute to, or inhibit, economic growth. With this background we can ask whether economies can grow forever, or whether the resulting changes in natural resources may constrain economic growth. A full understanding of the answer to this last question requires consideration of the social context within which land-use decisions take place. Accordingly, the last part of this chapter examines this interaction between economic and other social forces in determining the sustainability of economic growth, focusing particularly on land use and land-use patterns.

To Live Is to Alter

In today's advanced industrialized societies, some prominent environmentalists argue that we never should alter natural areas, that we should leave them "natural." Others tend toward the conservationist stance that we should use creation and maintain it over time so that future generations also may benefit from it. Still others argue that society should utilize creation as it sees fit, period. How does the economics of the Garden address this debate?

All living beings alter their environment. The act of breathing and maintaining a body of some sort requires the intake of matter and its transformation. So, we take in oxygen and breathe out carbon dioxide. We eat plants and animals and create waste products. The very state of being alive changes our environment. Beavers and buffalo exert great influences over their environment, creating lakes and maintaining prairies. If it weren't for them, the landscape would be quite different. So, if we wish to keep everything in a pristine unchanged state, we should eliminate life on the planet.

Of course, some people may argue that I have just destroyed a straw man. Instead, they would assert, we need to maintain life processes as they would be without people. After all, people change "nature." Similarly, many ecologists see humans as interlopers in the ecosystem, which would be much better off without them. Of course, this conflicts with the Garden's view of people as an intimate part of the natural system. People, being animals, change their environment just as beavers do. We merely seem to have a much greater capacity to alter the Garden than do other members of the enterprise. Indeed, people may play a determining role in causing areas we think of as natural to be what they are. For instance, tropical-forest dwellers tend to plant fruit trees, herbs, and other valuable plants around their villages, affecting the distribution of plants in the forest. What to the untrained eye appears to be pristine tropical rain forest, in many cases is a garden that people have manipulated for centuries. We often value as "pristine rain forest" something that people created in cooperation with ecological processes. Further north, the lower Little Tennessee River valley exhibits the effects of ten thousand years of native American settlements that displaced native species and created new habitats for species well adapted to exploiting human disturbances (Delcourt et al. 1986; cited in Hess 1992).[1] We either have to eliminate people, as Pogo once suggested, or we have to put up with their habit of Gardening.

If we humans wish to live as other than very "low impact" hunter-gatherers, we must alter natural systems at least somewhat and somewhere. For instance, if we live in an area with little population, swamps may provide excess waste treatment capacity while firm land may be scarce and highly prized. It could be perfectly rational, then, for us to drain some swamps to obtain some firm land as well as some agricultural food production. However, should we continue to drain swamps, waste-treatment functions would become increasingly valuable and firm-land functions less so.[2] We may lose irrevocably some goods and services of a particular swamp because we value them little compared to other things the land can provide or because we fail to realize what the system does. Even a society that cares about all species may lose some due to the impossibility of gathering sufficient ecological information to prevent their loss, or even to recognize their existence. The question then becomes one of how much to alter, not whether to alter at all.

Economists like to say that there is no free lunch—all things have a cost, as does altering natural systems to meet human needs. Changing the mix of goods and services provided by a natural system often carries a "switching cost," the costs incurred in the effort to alter the system. For instance, clearing the forest of trees to establish a farm represents the cost of switching the mix of goods from those provided by a later successional forest system to those provided by an early successional system. Preventing the fields from converting to a secondary forest requires outlays for weeding, a "maintenance cost." Other costs include opportunities we lose by not having the land as it was. Opportunity costs consist of the most valued thing(s) we give up by doing something. For instance, clearing a forest may cause us to lose soil retention and biodiversity. Society, therefore, pays for extra agricultural land with increased soil erosion and diminished biodiversity. Finally, cleared forests may cause erosion that negatively affects people downstream. Deforestation thereby imposes "external costs" on third parties, costs that upstream landowners normally do not have to pay. Of course, changing the natural system also may affect the persistence, resistance, and resilience of the system or certain of its functions. To the extent society loses these characteristics it pays another cost for changing Creation.

Natural Capital and Economic Growth

We have seen that living requires changing one's environment to some degree. When humans change natural systems, they pay a cost. What do these costs imply for the ability of economies to grow over time?

Perhaps we best can consider the process of economic growth by examining a portfolio of productive assets consisting of manufactured, natural, and human capital. Capital in the normal sense, "manufactured capital," consists of any long-lasting, manufactured resource used in the production and distribution of other goods and services. We use machinery, buildings, equipment, and inventory to produce and distribute goods and services and to get them to consumers. These are the "tools" with which society provides for itself. How inventory serves as a tool may require some explanation. Furniture manufacturers, for instance, may choose to maintain inventories of lumber, partially assembled furniture, and finished products. While doing so costs them money, having inventories on hand helps them through possible emergency situations. Should truckers go on strike, they can continue producing from their stores of lumber while they wait for the strike to end and new shipments to arrive. Should machinery break down, they can assemble semifinished chairs from their inventory and ship them while they make repairs. Or, should orders suddenly surge and strain the plant to its limits, manufacturers can fill surplus orders from the stock of finished furniture they have kept on hand against such an occurrence.

From an economic perspective, natural systems constitute natural capital. Natural systems, while not manufactured, do produce goods and services of use to people. Moreover, these systems share the critical characteristics of capital: durability and "sluggishness." Their durability links generations whereas their sluggishness implies that society cannot change instantly its stock of natural resources (the amount existing at a given time) any more than it can its stock of factories (Wilen 1985). Therefore, natural systems also are capital: natural capital.

In a similar vein, stocks of nonrenewables in the ground constitute an inventory of raw materials yet to be tapped. They provide us a stock of raw materials that we can draw upon whenever we need them. Thus, nonrenewable resources, too, represent natural capital.

Human capital consists of improvements in health, education, and skills that make humans more productive. Without human and manufactured capital humans cannot alter natural systems to provide the desired mix of products. Clearing a field requires human effort and tools. Thus, farmland represents a mixture of all three capitals. Similarly, without photosynthesis, water, mineral ores, and nutrient cycling, humans cannot produce manufactured and human capital. Manufactured capital provides goods and services that the ecosystem cannot. Human capital enables people to obtain more from a given amount of material or to use more effectively the functions offered by ecosystems. All three capitals interact and depend upon each other.

Figure 5.1 illustrates the interrelationships between the types of capital and between the capital portfolio and growth. The dark continuous lines represent flows of energy and matter. The dashed lines represent

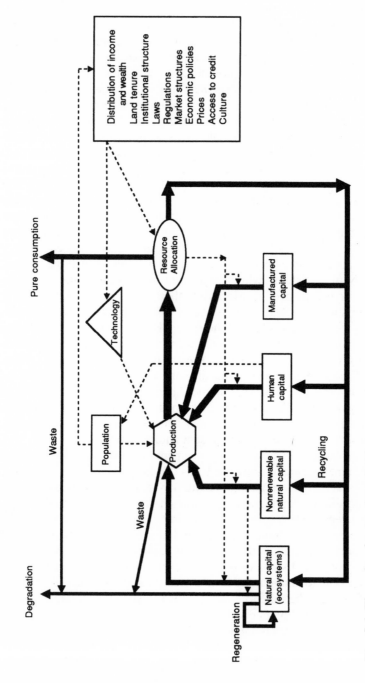

Fig. 5.1 The role of natural capital in economic processes

influences not characterized by flows of resources. Four blocks represent each of the capital stocks, including both kinds of natural capital. The flows out of the blocks into production represent depreciation, the use or depletion of capital by production. People deplete mineral deposits and degrade ecosystems. Human-energy reserves fall and machinery depreciates. These flows combine to produce goods and services. Production requires all three types of capital in various combinations depending upon the final goods and services produced and the technologies applied. Some goods such as autos may require large amounts of nonrenewable natural capital, whereas others such as education may require far more human capital than natural. Production, however, causes a drain on each form of capital to some degree. The way production uses the various capitals depends upon technology, which in turn depends upon the factors shown in the box on the right side of figure 5.1. The dashed arrow from technology to production shows the influence of technology on society's decision concerning the quantity of each type of capital to use in production.

The mix, amount, and use of goods and services produced by society greatly affect its ability to maintain or increase the level of production of goods and services by affecting the size of the capital stocks. Any addition to a stock of capital we consider investment. Society uses many goods for "pure" consumption that do not replenish any form of capital. Examples could include neckties, cheap novels, and perfumes. To varying degrees, however, consumption also may represent reinvestment in some form of capital. For instance, food consumption replaces worn-out human capital. Some food consumption may be pure consumption that does little for rebuilding the body (junk food). Other food consumption replaces worn-out muscle tissue and builds bones. Even the same food may represent both pure consumption and reinvestment. The gourmet meal does more than provide nutrition. To the extent that some of the resources used in producing it only provide transitory pleasure without rebuilding the body, to that extent the meal consists, in part, of pure consumption. Some medical care may represent pure consumption (some cosmetic surgery) whereas other medical care enables people to live more productive lives (setting broken bones). So, consumption represents a mix of pure consumption and reinvestment. The more that it consists of pure consumption, the less society adds to its capital portfolio. Society also adds to its capital portfolio directly by adding organic matter to the soil and planting windbreaks, recycling, replacing worn-out factories, and educating people. Ultimately, we can divide all production into two end uses: those that replace capital and those that do not. The two dark flows from "resource allocation" represent the division of the economy's output into pure consumption and reinvestment in capital. The dashed line from the box at the far right to "resource allocation" shows the influence of various socioeconomic factors on the decision as to how to divide its resources.

As society produces greater amounts of goods each year, it requires greater amounts of raw materials to make them. This implies more extraction of nonrenewable natural capital. Even recycling cannot totally overcome this fact because recycling is itself part of the production process—it also requires machinery, fuel, human capital, and so forth. So, production inevitably involves at least some extraction of natural resources. Note in figure 5.1 that in the case of renewable natural resources the arrow coming from the stock and returning to it represents additions resulting from natural regeneration.

Population enters the picture in several ways. Greater numbers of people require greater production, and therefore, more utilization of natural and other capital. Depending upon the population's standard of living, the rate of utilization of capital will be greater or smaller. The standard of living, of course, depends upon the rate of production vis-à-vis the size of the population. At the same time, if people have high levels of education, health care, and other forms of human capital, studies have shown that birth rates tend to fall. So, other things constant, higher levels of human-capital formation lead to lower levels of population. Debates over whether or not population growth causes environmental degradation sometimes miss the point. Population growth affects the environment, but the size of the impact depends upon the intensity with which that society utilizes resources and how it allocates them. Environmental change, in turn, can affect economic growth. Economic growth invested in human nutrition, education, and reforestation can lead to lower population growth with less environmental problems than the same economic growth devoted to consumption for a minority of the population. Concerns about population growth may be displaced—the actual problem may lie in the type of economic growth that is occurring. In other words, because population is part of a larger system, analyzing it in isolation leads to only a partial understanding of its role.

As people consume and produce, they inevitably create waste. These waste streams degrade renewable natural capital when the flow of waste from production and consumption exceeds the system's ability to assimilate it. The solid arrows from pure consumption and production to the leftmost flow out of renewable natural capital represent these waste flows. As the consumption of goods and services increases, so does the flow of waste and the outflow of renewable natural capital without its having served any productive purpose. The degree of environmental impact will depend upon the types of goods produced and the technology used in producing them. Waste treatment and recycling can reduce the flow of waste. Both activities, however, represent forms of "production" that, in turn, require the use of all forms of capital and that also generate waste. Recycling, for instance, requires people to expend human effort, fuel, and machinery to gather and sort waste, transport it to recycling centers for further crushing and baling, and then transport this processed waste to users. In the process, machinery wears out, machines consume gasoline and diesel, and exhaust fumes rise. While laudable, even recycling generates contaminants and consumes resources that could have been used for other purposes.

The above analysis shows us that the amount of depreciation of natural capital depends upon the amount of a society's production, its distribution throughout the populace, the size of the population, and the amount of reinvestment that occurs. Numerous socioeconomic factors affect the outcome. Even if recycling were aggressively pursued, however, some environmental degradation must occur. As Herman Daly (1974, 1980) points out, as the scale of economic activities occurs relative to the ecosystems that support it, the existence of wastes implies that society cannot escape environmental degradation, or declining natural capital.

Persistent Growth and Resources

Given that natural capital will be degraded at least to some degree by economic growth, many people ask whether the economic system can continue to provide higher and higher standards of living, or even whether it can maintain a given standard of living indefinitely. Much of the debate as to whether or not economies can grow forever without encountering limits has to do with technological change and the substitutability of manufactured capital for nonrenewable capital: will nonrenewable resources run out as growth proceeds?

Many mainstream, or neoclassical, economists tend toward "optimism." They point out that prices should rise as a certain material such as iron ore becomes scarcer, thereby encouraging technological change, the substitution of other materials for the ore, and more efficient utilization of the latter. While ore might become physically scarce, it might not become economically scarce—the higher prices lead to less use over time. Various authors have tested this hypothesis and generally have found that up to 1970, most materials have not become economically scarce over time. That is, it appears that they have not become more costly over time (the exact measure of cost, and even the adequacy of the cost approach, is a matter of debate). Some more recent studies indicate that some raw materials *have* become more costly since the 1970s. Whether or not technological change will respond sufficiently in the future to offset growing physical scarcity, even if it has in the past, remains a matter of conjecture. So, whether or not market processes can prevent growing physical scarcity of raw materials from slowing growth remains to be seen (Barnett and Morse 1963; Brown and Field 1978, 1979; Barnett 1979; Hall and Hall 1984).

Some economists, the "pessimists," believe that the above process will not work in the future even if it has in the past. Their concerns have to do with the risks inherent in depending upon technological change as an answer to growing physical scarcity. Howe (1979) points out that the institutional framework within which past technological change has occurred has itself changed greatly. He asks whether the framework can support the massive technological breakthroughs that will be needed. Smith and Krutilla (1977) suggest that technological change has relied on the use of the environment's ability to assimilate waste, so that much of the economic growth attributed to the growth of intangible inputs such as education and technology instead should be attributed to increased use of creation's self-cleansing ability. Accordingly, society may have to depend less on technological change as a partial solution to future resource scarcity. It can be added here that technological change itself often implies further depletion of nonrenewable resources and more environmental degradation because technological change usually is embodied in manufactured capital.

Many economists point out that, in order to compensate future generations for having less nonrenewable resources, present generations have to hand on to the future sufficient manufactured capital to offset the growing physical scarcity. Society does this to the extent that owners of nonrenewable resources take the returns or "profits" they receive from selling resources and convert much or all of these returns into new manufactured capital (Solow 1974a, 1974b).[3]

Page (1977) examines the above issues in terms of risk passed on to future generations. He points out that there is a difference between stating that nonrenewable resource extraction *can* benefit future generations (via manufactured capital formation) and that it *will* do so, inasmuch as in the United States about 90 percent of all raw-material extraction is used for short-lived consumer goods.[4] In addition, as non-renewable resource extraction continues, and at a faster rate, the future receives greater risks due to less resource availability and greater wastes inherited. Future generations must depend on technology to overcome a smaller resource base and therefore face increased risk that the needed technology will not be produced or developed in time. Moreover, technological change often carries with it, particularly today, uncalculated and perhaps unmanageable side effects.

To the above considerations we need to add the impacts of resource extraction on natural systems, the other type of natural capital. Extracting minerals from the earth inevitably causes some damage to natural systems. Therefore, we cannot ask only whether or not technology and prices can enable society to adapt successfully to declining stocks of nonrenewable natural capital. The declining stocks of nonrenewable resources also imply declining stocks of natural capital, unless society reinvests scarce resources back into protecting or regenerating these natural systems. We must ask whether or not society can adapt successfully to declining stocks of both kinds of capital.

Of course, if society can adapt successfully to declining nonrenewable resource stocks and human and manufactured capital can replace lost renewable natural capital, then humans do not have to worry. However, is the latter possible? Natural systems recycle nutrients such as nitrogen, provide the water cycle that produces rain, streams and groundwater, and give us the oxygen we breath. If it were possible for humans to use human ingenuity and manufactured capital to provide these services artificially, by living in a totally human-made, human-controlled environment, doing so might provide less human welfare, and certainly less welfare for all creation, than many would prefer. What would be the cost to the economy, let alone to other creatures, of such an approach? Surely as growth proceeds, more and more precious resources will have to be utilized to provide the basic environmental "infrastructure" or life-support system that used to be provided free of charge by creation. This implies that fewer resources will be available to supply consumers' direct needs. People will have fewer hamburgers, transportation, and television, as well as less human and manufactured capital to produce them. People will pay an opportunity cost for depreciating natural capital. The standard of living, accordingly, should suffer. Reliance on human and manufactured capital to substitute for continually declining natural systems ultimately implies that people will live in totally artificially constructed environments such as domes or colonies on the moon. Domed environments may be possible—but are they preferable? Do such environments represent the work of a caring, self-sacrificing gardener? The Creator, the original gardener, provides sufficient oxygen for all creatures. Domed environments, a human creation, provide an unequal distribution of oxygen—just enough for humans and too little for the rest of creation.

Because the amount of natural capital tends to decline as manufactured capital increases, the conditions for continued, or persistent, growth of consumption per person appear to become rather strict. At a minimum it would appear to require converting into manufactured capital a (perhaps substantial) proportion of the returns not only of nonrenewable resources but also of natural systems in order to offset, at least partially, the lost nonrenewable resources and the lost productive capacity of natural systems. This proportion probably would increase as the amount of natural capital declines and becomes relatively more essential. Even if this compensation were to occur, manufactured capital generally has a much shorter life than most natural systems that, depending on their utilization, may persist for long periods of time and repair themselves when damaged, as when forests recover from a storm. Thus, manufactured capital, though in some cases more valuable than a given natural system, may provide productive capacity for a shorter time.[5]

Landscapes and Persistent Economic Growth

Natural capital occurs in space. This spatial dimension matters greatly when we consider questions of the "sustainability" of economic processes. When we consider what a garden looks like, we realize that it is a natural system spatially ordered by a gardener to meet certain ends, including aesthetic and spiritual (such as in monastic and Japanese tea gardens). A good gardener knows that certain plants, when planted together, keep down weeds and insects. Some plants add beauty, if not economic gain, so some gardens contain sections or borders of flowers. Gardeners (particularly in the tropics) may include forests in their garden to provide sources of building material, beneficial insects, medicinal and food plants, animal protein, and water.[6] Gardens possess spatial orderings that make them successful in meeting various goals.

Landscapes, too, represent gardens where plants and animals interact in smaller natural systems (ecosystems) that, in turn, interact with other ecosystems on a larger scale. As seen above, depending upon the size, shape, and connectivity of the components of this large garden, their interrelationships make the landscape more or less useful for producing certain goods and services, maintaining biodiversity, and providing spiritual nourishment for humans. Landscapes where humans are present represent gardens created by a few or many gardeners.

Most societies wish to avoid risk and uncertainty. This requires establishing economy-sustaining landscapes that maintain natural functions, provide flexibility, preserve options, and provide resilience and resistance to disruption.[7] Doing so may require keeping options open. This may imply keeping natural systems sufficiently intact in a landscape that, should society come to desire the goods and services they provide, the landscape can change to provide these goods and services. Draining all the wetlands of a once-swampy area or removing all natural forest seed stock, for instance, may well foreclose producing badly needed goods and services those systems could offer at some time in the future. Prudence counsels maintaining sufficient swamps or forest reserves with the necessary spatial relationships to allow them to function well. (The difficulty of maintaining such desirable landscapes is discussed below.)

Similarly, maintaining sufficient individuals to perpetuate a species requires maintaining patches of habitat sufficient to meet the requirements of that species. Because some animal species migrate up and down slopes or rivers, or over large ranges, large tracts of land or dispersed patches connected by corridors may be required if humans are to maintain many animals. Similarly, many plant species require patches with large interior spaces.

Because living implies altering, society must choose how much to alter the landscape. Just as gardeners must choose how much land to clear for a garden, and where to place flowers and forests, so must society choose how to configure its landscape. A well-managed, landscape-level garden would contain some areas kept in a preserved state. These could be used, perhaps, for low-intensity recreation and places to get in touch with creation and biodiversity. They would be surrounded by buffer areas in which people use the land sustainably and maintain many of the ecological properties of the preserve. Outside the buffer areas people would employ land more intensively for urban use or agriculture. Preserves and their buffers would constitute patches sufficiently large to maintain the ecological integrity of entire ecosystem types and watersheds. Riparian zones, which connect land to water and upstream to downstream, would receive protection. They also could serve as corridors connecting preserves and their buffers. The landscape would be a mosaic of large, interconnected patches that maintain the ecological integrity of watersheds and that provide the option at some future date of returning intensively used land to much of its former state. As such, the landscape would resemble a well-designed garden that provides a good life for humans and nonhumans alike. Just as forests can constitute part of tropical gardens, so do wild areas constitute part of landscape gardens.[8]

The stability (persistence, resilience, and resistance) of a desirable landscape structure depends upon human as well as ecological factors. Humans bring their complex mosaic of institutions, cultures, and activities into the landscape's mosaic where the two patchworks interact. Thus, much of ecological stability has to do with how social organizations such as land tenure, property rights, and other institutional structures affect the landscape's structure. When many small landowners exist, a different landscape mosaic may occur than when a few large landowners hold the land. In the former case, gardens, woodlots, fields, windbreaks, fence lines, and hedgerows may create a patchwork quilt on the landscape whereas in the latter, large tracts of unbroken forest, sugarcane, corn, or other crops may result. The small and large landowners will respond differently to economic forces, such as changes in crop prices, and institutional changes, such as revisions of forestry laws. Thus, the landscape pattern itself may be more or less stable depending upon the landownership patterns and the environment within which they exist.[9] In turn, as shown above, the ecological stability of the landscape depends greatly on the mosaic resulting from land-use patterns.

We have seen that societies depend upon natural capital for economic processes, and that economists debate whether or not economies maintain sufficient natural capital to assure stable economic well-being. However, most of this debate ignores the spatial dimension of natural capital. Is it likely society will produce sufficient natural capital in an adequate spatial configuration to meet the requirements for sustainable growth, growth that is persistent, resistant, and resilient? In other words, because much natural capital exists within a landscape, will society produce landscapes that meet the above criteria?[10]

The Social Causes of Landscape Structure

To address this question we need to address the factors that affect land-use decision-making and land-use patterns. Figure 5.2 presents a scheme to guide our discussion. Market forces (such as prices and changes in incomes), the innermost circle, guide individuals to use land

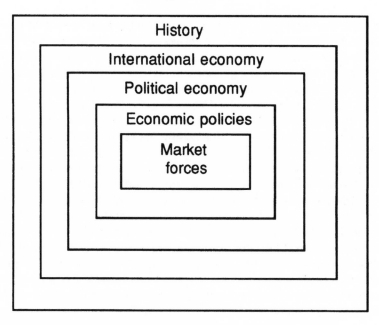

Fig. 5.2 Influences on landscape design

in certain ways. However, these decisions occur within a context that transcends pure demand and supply. Economic policies exert great control over local land-use decision making, as does the policy environment established by the interplay of politics and economics at the national level. International forces influence national economies and politics while history affects the current nature of both international and national factors impacting land use. Understanding the social factors that mold landscape structures requires us to investigate the forces operating at each level of analysis. We will start with market forces at the local level.

Market Forces

Economic theory states that, as the prices of the products of the land change, landowners choose those uses that provide the greatest return. For instance, on the urban fringe, farmers must decide whether to continue farming or to sell to a developer who will convert the farm into homes or a shopping center. The farmer decides by comparing two sums of money: the amount he would receive from selling the land and the "present value" of the land in agriculture. The latter represents the amount of money that, if put in the bank, would produce a stream of income over the years equivalent to what he would get from farming the land. If the amount of money the developer offers exceeds the present value of the land in agriculture, the farmer sells. In theory, the land moves to its "highest and best use," the use that provides society the highest return.

Applying this perspective in practice requires us to consider other factors that determine the prospective returns owners perceive and the way that they manage the land. Personal income plays an important role in affecting land use. People living on the edge of survival often must make land-use decisions that lower the risk of starvation now, even should this imply lower returns, lower yields, and less food in the future. They may farm steep slopes and resist establishing terraces that cost precious resources now but maintain yields over time. Despite facing severe losses in yields as erosion decreases their natural capital, they can ill afford the investment, though highly profitable, that terraces represent. Others living on the margin of survival do not feel that they can change technologies for fear of risking their families' lives. New crops or methods of raising animals, for instance, may promise higher income. Unless farmers can know for sure that the higher incomes will result, the new technology simply may be too risky to adopt. Similarly, farmers lacking secure access to land avoid improving the land for fear of losing the fruits of their effort to others. For this reason many such farmers resist using land for forestry because the returns from trees come so far in the future. Poor farmers need income now and cannot risk putting time and money into a long-lived investment when they might lose the land tomorrow.

The distribution of income and the land tenure system together greatly influence land use. These determine whether many or few live on the land and whether those living on the land own, rent, sharecrop, or merely work as landless laborers. The size of holdings, access to land, and quality of land available to different groups influence their income and the way they use their land. Large ranches and plantations may force rural populations into densely settled enclaves. Dense populations with insufficient land migrate to virgin territories, move onto marginal land such as hillsides, and decrease fallow periods between crops. Poor farmers may live off of their natural capital because they have few viable options, thereby degrading land under their control.

Lack of knowledge, a common companion to poverty, also affects the way people use land. Due to inadequate research and extension services, particularly in Third World countries, many farmers lack sufficient information about alternative practices that might serve them, and the environment, well. Many people, including landowners, also fail to realize the valuable functions played by natural systems. If resource owners were able to charge for these goods and services, they often would fail to do so out of ignorance. (We shortly will discuss why landowners often cannot charge for ecological goods and services.) If they did attempt to charge, users often would not pay, believing that they don't need natural systems' goods and services. Consequently, people fail to use land in ecologically benign, or at least more profitable, ways because people do not realize options available to them or value the critical ecological goods and services that land provides.

Cultural factors sometimes preclude people acknowledging certain land-use options. In many parts of Latin America, agriculture revolves around cattle, an attitude stemming from the Spanish culture of the colonists. Attempts to encourage tree farming or management of natural forests run up against biases against trees. Forested land is considered "unproductive," land that should be cleared to make way for cattle. In other areas, descendants of African slaves may resist attempts to get them to farm because farming to them carries connotations of slavery.[11]

So far we have examined how people decide to use land based upon their perceptions of the returns and risk of the alternatives available to them. Normally we would expect that such rational calculations would lead to efficient choices of land use. Economists believe, however, that, even if people had adequate information with which to make informed decisions, the market would fail to use land efficiently due to the existence of open-access resources, public goods, and externalities.[12]

Because no one owns clams on the beach, people assume that, in a sense, everyone does. By that they mean that clams constitute fair game. Whoever wants to take them may do so at their pleasure. Economists call whales, clams on the beach, clean air, and other such "unowned" goods "open-access property." Because everyone has access to the clams and no one pays for producing them, clams soon disappear. I know that, although I would be willing to restrain my clam digging to assure clams for the future, I cannot keep you from taking as many clams as you want. So, I dig them now before you take them all. Because we all do this, soon no one gets any. The same thing happens to whales. If whalers had to pay a fee for the services of the ocean in providing whales, their costs would be much higher and they would take far fewer whales. This "property rights perspective" shows that the lack of clearly defined ownership of environmental commodities and services lies at the root of many environmental problems. Because no one's legal rights are infringed upon when degradation occurs, no one has to pay for the degradation. So, people overuse creation. Of course, if everyone felt "ownership" of creation, that is, acted as gardeners caring for it, interior restraint could replace property rights! Regardless, no one receives payments for the economically valuable services of whales or of many of the valuable outputs of natural systems, so no one can reinvest a proportion of these returns to benefit future generations.

Ambiguity of ownership extends to "public goods," the second market failure. When providing a certain amount of a good to one person automatically provides that same quantity to everyone else in the market, economists call that good a "public good." One person's consumption of national defense does not deplete the amount of national defense available to others—I cannot prevent others from benefiting from my purchasing defense. Adam Smith argued that the government, not firms, should provide national defense because anyone purchasing an army to protect him- or herself against invasion automatically provides that same defense to everyone else. Similarly, no matter how much I look at the Great Smoky Mountains from afar others can look at them as much as they want. My observing the Smokies does not diminish the view for others (walking in them, however, may affect others' ability to enjoy them). Vistas of the Smokies, then, also constitute public goods.

The market cannot adequately provide such public goods because potential buyers for antimissile systems or scenic vistas wait for others to buy the good first. That way they obtain the benefits of these goods without paying for them—the "free rider" problem. Everybody waits for others to buy first, so that no one buys them at all. Accordingly, the market cannot provide sufficient public goods, whether national defense or beautiful views.

Not only does the market underproduce these goods, but because no one pays for them, no one can reinvest the returns from them. So, when a landowner's forest land produces water purification services for downstream users, she or he cannot sell these services to the beneficiaries because they all free ride. Consequently, she or he undervalues the forest providing the service and sees no need to reforest pasture that would clean water further—she or he does not reinvest returns from natural capital in more natural capital.

Public goods represent the extreme case of what are called "positive externalities." Externalities represent the third cause of market failure.

Positive externalities consist of side benefits accruing to third parties as the result of someone's doing something. If I get a flu shot, others receive better health, too, because they won't catch the flu from me. Yet, they received the benefits without asking for them or paying for them.

Negative externalities, on the other hand, exist when people engaged in some activity, such as cigar smoking or farming, have a negative impact on others but do not compensate them for this impact. Consider the case of a paper factory dumping chemicals into a river. The factory does not take into account the loss of income to shrimpers who depend upon clean water for their source of shrimp because these social costs lie outside of the factory's costs of production it must cover. This situation exists because of a lack of rights to chemical-free water. Shrimpers cannot sue the upstream factory for damages because the law often fails to state clearly that shrimpers have the right to clean water. The lack of clearly defined rights to environmental quality leads to many forms of environmental degradation.[13] By not requiring the factory to bear all the costs it inflicts on society, the returns to paper production appear artificially high, causing too many acres of land to be converted to paper factories.

Similarly, because owners of wetlands do not get paid for the positive externalities their land provides (such as water-quality maintenance and fish-hatchling production for offshore fisheries), the return to wetlands appears artificially low and too many wetlands get filled in for housing and other development.

Typically economists call for systems of subsidies and fines to deal with externalities. When landowners cause positive externalities, society would pay them for the extra benefits they produce. Similarly, landowners who pollute would pay a tax or fine equal to the extra cost they impose on members of society. These payments cause landowners to "internalize the externalities," to take these external benefits or costs into account in their decision making and thereby to correct the failure of the market to make efficient land-use decisions.[14]

According to Coase (1960) government need not intervene to create a system of subsidies and taxes because individuals would do so on their own if property rights are well defined. He argues that in this case, the presence of externalities does not cause the market to fail. If polluters had the right to pollute, individuals would pay polluters money (up to the amount of damages individuals received) not to pollute. If individuals had the right to a pollution-free environment, polluters would pay individuals for permission to discharge waste. Either way, the "optimal" amount of pollution would occur. In reality, however, these compensatory payments rarely occur because too often so many polluters and victims are involved that it is difficult to know (1) who is causing the damage, (2) how much damage each polluter causes, and (3) who is being hurt by pollution. The cost of obtaining the information and organizing all the payments (the "transaction cost") is so high that the transactions do not occur. In these cases, economists argue that government should intervene if it can do so with sufficiently low costs to justify the benefits that would result.

To the above catalog of three market failures we must add a fourth, only recently recognized, market failure—the presence of "economies of configuration." As we have seen, the goods and services a landscape provides depends upon its spatial pattern of land covers and uses. Individual landowners together produce this pattern while being largely ignorant of the ecological relationships that they are affecting. These effects may occur over long time periods and distances, making understanding the ecological impacts of land-use decisions even more difficult.

The typical response of using subsidies and taxes to deal with externalities in this situation fails for three reasons. First, the very high transaction costs involved over most landscapes precludes individuals from internalizing externalities and creating socially desirable landscapes. Second, government attempts to intervene would require intensive knowledge about each landowner's potential contribution to the landscape under all potential configurations in order to assess the correct subsidy or tax. Even if such knowledge were possible (generally it is not at this point in time), this intensive micromanagement lies beyond the ability and funds of most governments, particularly when we consider all of the landscapes in a country's territory. Third, using standard taxes and subsidies to internalize standard externalities cannot achieve socially desired landscape mosaics because of scale problems. Because landowners jointly determine the landscape's configuration, attempts to optimize land-use patterns must deal with landowners as a group, for it is at this scale that landscape level processes emerge, not at the individual level.

Accordingly, individual owners acting alone cannot provide the socially optimal mix of ecologically provided goods and services, nor can typical internalizing of externalities. In short, the presence of economies of configuration implies that the market will fail, even when traditional methods of internalizing externalities are applied. Other means have to be found to deal with landscape-scale ecological processes (Wear 1992; Gottfried et al. 1994a).

The Context for Market Forces

We have seen that markets guide land use by affecting the returns to land, owners' income, and perceived risk. Markets frequently fail to yield best land-use patterns due to problems of open-access resources, public goods, externalities, and economies of configuration. However, people make decisions on how to use land within the context of economic policies, a political economic system, an international economy, and a particular set of historical circumstances (see figure 5.2). We need to examine each of these influences in turn in order to understand better what determines land use. Then we can address the likelihood that land-use patterns will yield sufficent natural capital in the necessary spatial configurations to provide persistent, resistant, and resilient economic growth.

Economic policies play a large role in affecting land-use patterns by affecting the relative returns from different land uses and the interest rate. As examples, consider the following. When central banks raise and lower interest rates to control the economy, they make interest-sensitive industries such as home construction and modern capital-intensive farming more or less profitable, affecting in turn how land-owners use the land. Rising property taxes due to growing urbanization in the United States may force out farmers who cannot afford them while land taxes in northern Africa promote cash cropping to bring in foreign exchange. Subsidies for fertilizers, gasoline, and tractors make modern agriculture more profitable than it would be otherwise in many countries, prompting farmers to cultivate larger areas, including marginal, easily degraded terrain. Overvalued exchange rates lower agricultural prices to Third World farmers, driving them to the cities where they hope to find higher incomes.[15] Macroeconomic policies and international trade policies affect prices, thereby affecting the crops farmers plant, the rate of farm conversion to urban uses, and the rate of colonization of new lands or abandonment of rural areas. In all these ways, economic policies affect landscape patterns.

As shown in figure 5.2, the political economic environment exerts much influence on how land-use decisions are made and on who makes them. First, the ownership of resources and the subsequent distribution of income affect who makes the decisions on behalf of whom; that is, the political system. In a centralized economic system, such as the former Soviet Union, the state owns the land and the elite determine how to use it by means of a complex bureaucracy watched over by an ever-present party. Peasants work state farms or farm state land in collectives that make decisions. However, farmers' decision making depends greatly upon policies imposed by the central government. In the former Soviet Union, the government emphasized heavy industry over agriculture, so that agriculture received relatively little support. In a market economy with land owned by many land users, democratic decision-making processes tend to prevail so that landowners' interests influence the institutions that affect their self-interest. Thus U.S. agricultural policy such as price supports (expressed through a decentralized ownership and decision-making system) tends to favor farmers more than in the former Soviet centralized system.

The environment of institutions, regulations, and market structures resulting from the political system and the distribution of income and power bias landowners toward certain land uses and away from others. The presence of supportive or regulatory government agencies, credit institutions, and cooperatives affects the profitability and feasibility of various land uses. Large landowners can influence the government to offer subsidized loans for large cattle operations, a policy that benefits them immensely while benefiting subsistence farmers little. By raising the profitability of such operations, these programs encourage deforestation and the concentration of land in fewer hands. Insecure tenancy arrangements and poor access to credit may cause landowners to shy away from long-term investments in land and instead seek to "cash in" the natural capital (forests, minerals, animals) on the land as soon as possible. Even well-intended, environmentally oriented laws banning the export of tropical hardwoods from a Third World country can depress local wood prices so that no one will consider using land for sustainable forestry operations.

International economic forces work their way into the landscape by affecting the profitability of different crops and natural resources, and the incomes of the groups of people who own those resources. When international agreements to regulate the price of bananas and coffee successfully raise these prices and prevent them from fluctuating wildly, landowners more likely will use land for these crops. However, when these agreements falter, farmers may abandon coffee and banana plantations or convert them to other uses. Free-trade agreements, such as NAFTA, may lower the price of some crops and raise others. NAFTA should produce lower corn and bean prices for Mexican subsistence farmers who cannot compete with U.S. farmers. Yet, NAFTA may allow large Mexican landowners who receive water from government-built irrigation projects better access to U.S. markets for their vegetables. The U.S. farmers who export to Mexico or who compete against Mexican vegetables similarly stand to gain and lose. Trade agreements aside, as Brazilian farmers increase soy and orange production, these products enter the U.S. market and affect farmers' decision making here. Minerals and forest products face similar pressures and opportunities. Hence, the forces of international trade can affect strongly the returns to various land uses and to the owners of natural resources, thereby changing the nature of landscapes.

Finally, history also affects present land use. Colonial land grants given to the conquistadors in Latin America continue today in the large estates, or latifundia, that dominate agriculture there. Similarly, when the Guatemalan government confiscated German-owned coffee plantations at the end of World War II, these plantations became government-owned coffee plantations within a largely free-market economy. In another part of the world, the U.S. government bought thousands of acres of heavily degraded, poor quality farmland covering denuded mountains in an effort to improve the water quality in southern Appalachia. This formed the basis for southern national forests that dominate the landscapes and economies of many southern areas. Similarly, at the turn of the century, many large U.S. and foreign companies bought large tracts of inexpensive forest land for their forest and mineral wealth. Large expanses of commercially exploited forest, wilderness, and recreation-oriented forest areas have resulted from these acquisitions. Current land use, therefore, depends to a greater or lesser extent on land use and landownership in the past.

As we have seen above, the spatial design of landscapes depends upon a multitude of factors such as market forces, policies, the intertwining of politics and economics, international forces, and history. The decision as to how to utilize natural capital occurs in this context. No mechanism exists to determine the correct scale of economic activity relative to the ecosystems that support it. More precisely, no guarantee exists that a society will produce landscape patterns, nor particular land uses, that will provide the mix of goods and services that the society desires from natural capital, nor the correct amount of natural capital. Neither can a people be sure that the resulting landscapes will prove resistant and resilient. Without their being aware of their doing so, land users' interactions provide a public good—the resistance and resilience of the landscape. Yet, there exists no mechanism for land users to provide the amount of that public good that they, and others, desire. Thus, the market fails to allocate land efficiently between the various uses to which it can be put. It overexploits natural capital and underproduces resistance and resilience.

For an example of how the above factors combine to determine land use and the sustainability of economic activity in a region, let us turn to the example of the Osa Peninsula of Costa Rica.

Case Study: Deforestation in the Osa Peninsula of Costa Rica

Costa Rica, the site of the Rio summit's Earth Council, currently suffers the highest deforestation rate in Central America.[16] During the 1980s Costa Rica lost 7.6 percent of its forests per year (Hartshorn et al. 1982; Bilsborrow 1991). Whereas originally 99.8 percent of Costa Rica was forested, the country's forests now cover less than one-third of its area. More than half of the deforestation has occurred since 1950 (Hartshorn et al. 1982). This deforestation affects more than Costa Ricans. It has been estimated that at least 15 percent of the 1,500 tree species screened so far in Costa Rica could be useful in treating cancer (Leonard 1987). Costa Rica's natural capital is rapidly depreciating.

The Osa Peninsula, which contains the largest remaining rain forest on the Central American Pacific coast, shares both its country's richness and its deforestation. Ecologists have estimated that over 750 species of trees exist on the Osa, which is marked by a high degree of endemism; that is, a large percentage of its species are restricted to or native to this region. The Golfo Dulce Forest Reserve contains 61,350 hectares (approximately 40 percent of the peninsula) that serve as a buffer around Corcovado National Park, the crown jewel of Costa Rica's national park system. However, because in essence the reserve is an open-access resource, people already have cut approximately one-third of the reserve's forest cover. During the late 1980s the reserve lost about 5 percent of its forest cover per year.

The eight thousand residents of the forest reserve consist of low-income people who have migrated into the area from the southwestern Pacific region. Typically they survive by selling timber and then utilizing the cleared land for agriculture and cattle. However, the steep slopes, fragile soils, and high precipitation render most reserve lands unsuitable for either crops or cattle. After two to three years of crops, the yields fall to such low levels that the farmers must clear new land and begin again.

The development of the Osa currently has proceeded under a model that mixes the free market with substantial government intervention. Of the 150,000 hectares on the peninsula about 88 percent fall within protected areas administered by the Osa Conservation Area (ACOSA), an organization of the Costa Rican Ministry of Natural Resources, Energy and Mines (MIRENEM). Within the reserve the Institute for Agrarian Development (IAD) administers 20,000 hectares. However, the four hundred farmers who either are squatters, beneficiaries or grantees actually control the use of that land. Their parcels range from 5 to 300 hectares in size. In the 41,000 hectares of the non-IAD portion of the reserve only 5 percent of properties have clear deeds. While land use effectively rests in private hands, legal rights reside with the government to a large degree while the Costa Rican Forestry Service (DGF) regulates the use of the forests on these lands. Therefore, while landholders may exert much effective control over land use, they are constrained by the legal system and the DGF.

Why do peasants on the Osa insist on cutting trees when their long-term welfare depends upon the forest? One of the main reasons consists of the need to survive. The people who migrate to the Osa come to farm. They see this frontier as a beacon of opportunity. Few consider forestry as a possible source of income because relatively little tradition of managing forests for profit exists in Costa Rica. So, legally or illegally, farmers clear land to do what they know how to do—grow crops and raise cattle. For them, trees represent an obstacle to obtaining income. As one farmer, now a confirmed "environmentalist," told the author: "I used to go out and cut the trees with my chainsaw. How I used to love to hear them *fall*." Farmers sell the marketable timber to loggers at a low price and clear the remainder of the land for agriculture. Because most of the timber is shipped to locales 200–400 kilometers away, landholders receive only about $65 per tree.

Even farmers wishing to manage their land as a money-making forestry operation encounter several obstacles. The well-intentioned DGF, and the laws establishing it, impose strict regulation of forest activities. In this way the government hopes to stem the deforestation and ensure forest cover. However, this regulation represents a two-edged sword for the environment. While regulations are intended to ensure proper management of land and to slow deforestation, they raise the costs of managing a sustainable timber-producing operation. The DGF requires detailed management plans beyond the ability, comprehension, and income of the typical peasant. These plans identify the location of potentially marketable trees and indicate when they will be harvested and the location of logging roads. Once peasants file their plans, they must apply annually for permission to cut the trees specified in the plan. Due to the bureaucratic nightmare and delays involved in developing a plan and obtaining permits, the lack of forestry extension assistance, and the insufficiently trained Forest Service staff that turns over with every change of party, forest management entails high costs.

Forestry in Costa Rica resembles farming in a country that requires farmers to plan in advance exactly what crops they will plant, how they will plant them, and when they will harvest and how. A professional agronomist must draw up the plan. Then the farmer must go to the capital, perhaps a full day's trip away, to secure approval of the plan. Upon arriving at the office the farmer learns that the plan lacks the proper signatures or that the "plan approval officer" will not be in the office until next week. After three trips to the capital he receives approval for the plan. Then, every year he must repeat the process to gain permission to harvest. Unfortunately, the permits usually arrive too late to permit harvesting most of the crop. It is hard to imagine that anyone would choose to farm under such conditions. Yet, Costa Rican landowners face these same problems should they choose to enter forestry. Accordingly, few do.

Because landholders on the Osa usually lack secure title, they have no guarantee of receiving the returns on their efforts. Why should a peasant invest time and scarce money for returns that come in over many years when she may lose her land next year? In this situation the rational peasant clears the land now and gets what money she can while the opportunity to do so still exists. She understands agriculture and knows the returns from it. Meanwhile, uncertainty and high cost lower the returns to the little-known and, therefore, risky forest alternative relative to those from agriculture. Faced with quick, more-certain returns, the peasant chooses agriculture over forestry.

A well-intentioned law banning the export of tropical hardwood logs from the country also depresses the revenue earned from forest management. The national legislature passed the law in an attempt to curb the excessive rate of cutting in the country. However, the law means that the price of a log, which normally would be determined according to international demand and supply, falls to the lower domestic price level. As a result, precious hardwoods end up as domestically produced low-quality plywood or construction timber instead of furniture. Landholders receive low prices for their trees because the end product also sells for low prices. If landholders could sell logs to high-quality furniture producers, who usually reside abroad, forestry would provide much higher returns.

Government policies and institutions favor agriculture against forestry. Generous tax credits and low-interest loans for cattle production (the latter funded largely by foreign agencies) provide strong financial incentives to clear land for cattle. Whereas the DGF offers little forestry advice to landowners, the Ministry of Agriculture does offer agricultural extension services to landowners. Due to high costs, low revenues, lack of knowledge, and insufficient technical support for forestry, landholders opt to cut trees and replace them with "subsidized" cattle.

Finally, although the world might benefit from Costa Ricans' preserving the diversity of plant and animal life on the Osa, the Osa's residents cannot afford to do so because no one pays them to safeguard it. The residents produce a public good—biodiversity—and the rest of the world acts as a free rider. If the world benefits from the Osa's biodiversity but its residents pay for it by forgoing the income from farming, the Osa's peasants will have no choice but to farm. Equity and necessity both indicate that the world somehow should compensate Costa Ricans for preserving their biodiversity.[17]

The future appears bleak for the Osa's inhabitants. While the Golfo Dulce Forest Reserve possesses a large stock of renewable and nonrenewable natural resources, the region itself obtains little benefit from its rich natural capital that is rapidly depreciating. Individuals and firms harvest trees with little attention to the long-term economic consequences of these actions. They largely export the reserve's resources outside of the region, reinvesting few profits on the reserve to provide the basis for a higher, sustainable standard of living. This export model views forests purely as a source of raw materials, not as multiproduct assets capable of providing multiple benefits over a long period of time. Consequently, they underinvest in natural capital. The low returns to tree harvesting, the lack of social and economic infrastructure, and the poverty of the area mean that the residents invest their meager proceeds in little human or manufactured capital to offset the loss of natural capital.

As the deforestation proceeds, the reserve's forest probably will become more and more fragmented, comprising patches of smaller and smaller size with fewer and fewer corridors connecting them. This may have a variety of impacts on biodiversity, timber quality, and sedimentation rates. In addition, the size of the forest patch including the reserve and the Corcovado Park will decline, endangering species that require large ranges. Deforestation, therefore, will decrease the output of the various environmental goods and services produced by the peninsula's natural capital "free of charge." Moreover, since the great majority of the soils of the reserve will not sustain a productive, profitable agriculture, it will not provide the basis for a higher, sustainable standard of living when the forest is cleared. Because of economies of configuration, the market fails to produce socially desirable landscapes.

Furthermore, little may exist to attract outside-manufactured capital to the area once the forest is gone. Far from major markets, the Osa's hilly terrain complicates transportation while the relatively low population density offers few labor supply advantages. Capital would locate, if anywhere, on the coastal plain. Reserve residents then would have to commute, returning to their homes on weekends (unless they happened to have a car), or move. Also, because the capital on the coastal plain tends to be multinational, as in the case of the extensive palm oil, tree, and banana plantations, deforestation easily could make the reserve population dependent upon a foreign-dominated, export-driven model of development.

Due to an unfortunate combination of market forces, poverty, public goods, policies, laws, ignorance, and cultural values, the Osa may lose much of its natural capital without receiving other forms of capital in compensation, despite the valiant efforts of internationally sponsored projects located there. The open-access nature of the reserve, when combined with the lack of a coordinating mechanism between landowners, conspires to create suboptimal landscapes and overexploitation of the natural capital. The lack of forestry extension services and cultural attitudes tend to make residents not even consider forestry as a land-use option. Should they do so, the political economic environment tends to make forestry unattractive. As a result, higher standards of living for the Osa's current and future inhabitants, as well as the survival of many unique forms of life, may prove an elusive goal unless fundamental legal, technical, and administrative reforms occur.

Some Reflections and Conclusions

Due to the unclear nature of property rights for many natural systems and their products, the public-goods aspect of many natural-system functions, the fact that the returns to natural capital often go unrecognized and/or unclaimed, and the haphazard design of landscapes, it is unlikely that much reinvestment of the returns to natural capital will occur and that landscape patterns will be resilient and resistant. Society ends up with too little natural capital now because of overexploitation and future generations end up with too little compensation for the lower amount of natural capital they inherit.

As long as society relies on technological change and substitutability to serve as its saviors in the face of declining natural-capital stocks and of the lack of reinvestment, the future may prove rather bleak. Due to the extent of environmental degradation in most countries today prudent natural resource policy generally would minimize environmental disruption in order to maintain the natural capital base.[18] This would imply the need to minimize resource extraction through appropriate policies and through recycling. It also implies that society may find it appropriate to consider the level of material well-being to which it aspires and whether the demands implicit in that standard of living permit sustainable welfare over time. Finally, society also must consider how best to organize people so that land-use decision making incorporates the spatial dimensions of natural capital. These considerations raise issues about the meaning of sustainable development and about the characteristics of institutions most capable of achieving socially desirable landscapes. We will examine these concerns in the last chapter.

Faced with changing international trade patterns and markets, changes in tastes and products, possible new uses for genetic information stored in plants and animals, and untold new challenges from a rapidly evolving world, societies need to maintain a portfolio of natural assets against these contingencies and the physical and human assets capable of utilizing these assets fully. Societies wishing to improve the living conditions of their human members, as well as provide for the well-being of all of creation in an uncertain world, need to create a spatially ordered capital portfolio (natural, human, and manufactured) that provides persistent and stable productivity, and flexibility, the ability to respond to changing conditions. Doing so will require social institutions that facilitate the establishment of landscapes whose mosaics resist change, recover quickly from it, and provide flexibility in the face of an uncertain future. It also requires dealing with poverty and inequitable distribution of income and of access to resources.

Yet, no guarantee exists that humans will produce a mosaic that provides sufficient reserves to guarantee flexibility or to maintain the biological diversity of the system. The entire biophysical environment that nurtured human society can change to the point that society cannot survive. Sumer's downfall due to salinization, siltation, and critical wood shortages resulting from poor irrigation drainage, and deforestation, reminds us of the importance of this basic relationship (Eckholm 1976; Perlin 1989).

Professionals from many disciplines need to examine the spatial implications of resource use, starting at the local level and working up through the landscape and international scales. Unless policymakers understand how multiproduct natural capital interacts with people on the local and landscape levels, it will be difficult for them to formulate policies that address the welfare of the people and natural systems where they live. Similarly, they need to examine the impacts of local, regional, national, and international institutions on natural capital within a spatial context.

The failure to appreciate the importance of natural capital to human welfare leads to inefficiency, a cardinal economic sin. The cases of Poland and Costa Rica illustrate this point. It has been reported that due to environmental damage, Poland suffers a GNP 20 percent lower than it would have been otherwise (Nelson 1990). Similarly, according to the World Resources Institute, from 1970 to 1989 Costa Rica's forests, soils, and fisheries depreciated by more than $4.1 billion. Although the authors concede that the impact of this depreciation on development is difficult to determine with precision, a simple analysis shows that the growth of gross domestic product easily could have suffered a 25–30 percent loss as a result (Solórzano et al. 1991).

In light of the above discussion, we must conclude that the landscape mosaic and the allocation of resources between pure consumption and capital greatly determine the persistence of economic growth or of a given level of well-being. Market forces, history, social and political factors, and culture all combine to influence this allocation and mosaic. However, the discussion thus far misses a critical point, at least as far as the ancient Hebrews are concerned. We will turn to that point next.

Notes

1. Cited in (Hess 1992).

2. Chapter 4 defines ecological functions as goods and services that natural systems provide humans or other natural systems.

3. The technical term for such returns is "rents."

4. Much the same could be said for Third World countries' use of resource export earnings for luxury good imports, as Goodland and Ledec (1986) point out.

5. In his review of the neoclassical theoretical work on the sustainability of economic well-being (utility), Toman and his colleagues (1994) conclude that those who rely on technological change and on finding substitutes for natural capital draw comfort from the analyses that show the efficacy, under certain strict conditions, of these approaches. Others, however, question the realism of these conditions and, therefore, remain less optimistic. The authors state that one of the most important lessons from the literature is that sustainability does not necessarily follow from achieving efficiency, the latter understood as maximizing the present value of utility (individual well-being) over time. The total rate of savings as expressed in the amount of built capital and natural capital

may be too low, even when substitution and innovation possibilities are favorable. Given less favorable possibilities, maintaining natural capital becomes even more important. Accordingly, internalizing externalities (see the section above on market forces) and correcting market failures may prove necessary for sustainability, but not sufficient. They conclude that achieving sustainability may require collective action beyond market processes, a conclusion consistent with that of this book.

6. Traditional tropical gardens often resemble forests more than temperate gardens. See chapter 6 for more on tropical polyculture.

7. As stated in chapter 2, ecological functions persist when they maintain the same or greater level over time. Resistance implies that the functions of a natural system resist change. Ecologists state that resilient functions are those that bounce back after being disrupted by some outside disturbance. We may view sustainability, then, as maintaining or increasing desired traits even in the face of disruptions that threaten these traits.

8. Using protected areas as buffers to protect vital ecological processes and/ or species corresponds to the economic concept of "safe minimum standard" (Ciriacy-Wantrup 1952; Bishop 1978; Toman 1994). Society establishes safe minimum standards when uncertainty is high and the potential costs of some irreversible change, such as crossing an ecosystem threshold or decreasing an endangered species' habitat below a critical level, are high. Society only imposes the standard, which might limit tree harvesting or land clearing to a certain amount, when the costs of doing so are tolerable.

9. This hypothesis currently is being examined by a research project of the Temperate Zone Directorate of the U.S. Man and the Biosphere Program. Two papers study the impact of different owner types on landscape cover and change over time: Turner et al. (1994), "Influence of Land Ownership on Land-cover Change in the Southern Appalachian Highlands and the Olympic Peninsula"; and Wear et al. (1994), "Ecosystem Management in Multi-Ownership Setting." To obtain copies of these papers contact the principal investigator of the project, Dr. Robert Naiman, Center for Streamside Studies AR-10, University of Washington, Seattle, Wash. 98195.

10. Framing the question this way leads us to focus on renewable resources at the expense of nonrenewable resources. However, because the spatial dimension of the sustainability debate has been so widely ignored, I think the benefits of focusing on landscapes exceed the costs of doing so.

11. A Peace Corps volunteer, for instance, told the author that the Afro-Caribbean people with whom he worked in Belize resisted attempts to teach them agriculture. Because their slave ancestors had had to farm, they saw returning to agriculture as returning to slave conditions. The volunteer's project involved teaching agriculture in a secondary school.

12. For a more thorough discussion of these topics see any of the environmental economics texts in the further readings section at the end of the book.

13. Note that most economists would not argue that no chemicals at all

should be dumped into the river. After all, to live is to alter. Rather, they would state that vague laws make it difficult to achieve a socially desirable amount of pollution whereby the need of producers to deal with waste inexpensively is balanced against the cost to society of impure water.

14. This is the response of Pigou to the problem of externalities. More accurately, subsidies or taxes would equal the monetary value of the external benefit or cost of the last unit they produce when they are producing the optimal amount of production (or, the optimal amount of pollution). Today other approaches such as markets for permits to discharge pollutants into water or air also are being tested. See part 2 in Pearce and Turner (1990) for detailed discussions of these approaches.

15. International markets generally establish prices on agricultural products that are widely consumed. When governments set exchange rates for their currency at rates above what the market would set, this makes the price for that country's exports lower in terms of the domestic currency. For instance, assume the country of Zandunga sets its exchange rate at $1.00 per zan, the domestic currency, whereas the market rate is $0.50 per zan. If the international price of corn were $2.00 per bushel of corn, farmers would receive 4 zans for each bushel of corn they produced under the market-established exchange rate. However, with the overvalued exchange rate set by the government, they only would receive 2 zan. Governments often overvalue exchange rates in order to provide cheap imports for industrialization programs or urban elites. Inflationary conditions also lead to overvalued exchange rates, when the government sets the exchange rate and does not change it frequently enough to keep up with inflation.

16. This section draws heavily from material in Campos (1991) and Gottfried, Brockett, and Davis (1994).

17. Under the terms of the new Joint Implementation Treaty between the United States and Costa Rica, U.S. electric utility companies may compensate for their emissions of carbon into the atmosphere by paying Costa Ricans to plant trees or maintain forests, which capture atmospheric carbon. Exactly how this works out in practice, and how much it helps stem deforestation, remains to be seen.

18. Chapter 3 in Pearce and Turner (1990) develops this point particularly well.

References

Barnett, Harold J. 1979. ''Scarcity and Growth Revisited.'' Pp. 163–217 in *Scarcity and Growth Reconsidered*, ed. V. Kerry Smith. Baltimore: Johns Hopkins University Press.

Barnett, Harold J., and Chandler Morse. 1963. *Scarcity and Growth: The Economics of Natural Resource Availability*. Baltimore: Johns Hopkins University Press.

Bilsborrow, Richard. 1991. "Demographic Processes, Rural Development and Environmental Degradation in Latin America." Paper presented at Sixteenth Conference of the Latin American Studies Association, April 4–6, at Washington, D.C.

Bishop, Richard C. 1978. "Endangered Species and Uncertainty: The Economics of a Safe Minimum Standard." *American Journal of Agricultural Economics* 60(1): 10–18.

Brown, Gardner M., Jr., and Barry C. Field. 1978. "Implications of Alternative Measures of Natural Resource Scarcity." *Journal of Political Economy* 86(2): 229–44.

———. 1979. "The Adequacy of Measures for Signaling the Scarcity of Natural Resources." Pp. 218–48 in *Scarcity and Growth Reconsidered*, ed. V. Kerry Smith. Baltimore: John Hopkins University Press.

Campos, Jose J. 1991. "The BOSCOSA Project: Case Study of Sustainable Natural Resource Management and Community Development in the Osa Peninsula, Costa Rica." Paper presented at Humid Tropical Lowlands Conference: Development Strategies and Natural Resource Management. DESFIL, June 17–21, in Panama.

Ciriacy-Wantrup, Siegfried V. 1952. *Resource Conservation*. Berkeley: University of California Press.

Coase, Ronald. 1960. "The Problem of Social Cost." *Journal of Law and Economics* 3(October): 1–44.

Daly, Herman E. 1974. "The Economics of the Steady State." *American Economic Review* 64(2): 15–21.

———. 1980. "The Steady-State Economy: Toward a Political Economy of Biophysical Equilibrium and Moral Growth." Pp. 324–55 in *Economics, Ecology, and Ethics: Essays Toward Steady State Economy*, ed. Herman E. Daly. San Francisco: W. H. Freeman.

Delcourt, Paul A., Hazel R. Delcourt, Patricia A. Cridlebaugh, and Jefferson Chapman. 1986. "Holocene Ethnobotanical and Paleoecological Record of Human Impact on Vegetation in the Little Tennessee River Valley, Tennessee." *Quarternary Research* 25: 330–49.

Eckholm, Erik P. 1976. *Losing Ground: Environmental Stress and World Food Prospects*. New York: W. W. Norton.

Goodland, Robert, and George Ledec. 1986. "Neoclassical Economics and Principles of Sustainable Development." Washington, DC: Office of Environmental and Scientific Affairs, World Bank.

Gottfried, Robert R., Charles D. Brockett, and William C. Davis. 1994. "Models of Sustainable Development and Forest Resource Management in Costa Rica." *Ecological Economics* 9(2): 107–20.

Gottfried, Robert R., David Wear, and Robert Lee. 1994. "Landscapes, Ecosystem Value, and Sustainability." Presented at the 1994 Association of Environmental and Resource Economists Workshop, "Integrating the Environment and the Economy: Sustainable Development and Economic/Ecological Modeling," June 6, at Boulder, Colo.

Hall, Darwin C., and Jane V. Hall. 1984. "Concepts and Measures of Natural Resource Scarcity, with a Summary of Recent Trends." _Journal of Environmental Economics and Management_ 11(4): 363–79.

Hartshorn, Gary, Lynne Hartshorn, Agustin Atmella et al. 1982. "Costa Rica, Country Environmental Profile: A Field Study." (December). San José, Costa Rica: Tropical Science Center.

Hess, Karl, Jr. 1992. _Visions upon the Land._ Washington, DC: Island Press.

Howe, Charles W. 1979. _Natural Resource Economics: Issues, Analysis and Policy._ New York: John Wiley & Sons.

Leonard, H. Jeffrey. 1987. _Natural Resources and Economic Development in Central America: A Regional Environmental Profile._ New Brunswick, N. J.: Transaction Books for the International Institute for Environment and Development.

Nelson, Mark M. 1990. "Darkness at Noon." _Wall Street Journal,_ March 18.

Page, Talbot. 1977. _Conservation and Economic Efficiency._ Baltimore: Johns Hopkins University Press.

Pearce, David W., and R. Kerry Turner. 1990. _Economics of Natural Resources and the Environment._ Baltimore: Johns Hopkins University Press.

Perlin, John. 1989. _A Forest Journey: Wood and the Rise and Fall of Civilization._ Lincoln: University of Nebraska Press.

Smith, V. Kerry, and John V. Krutilla. 1977. _Resource and Environmental Constraints to Growth._ Washington D.C.: Resources for the Future.

Solórzano, Raúl, Ronnie de Camino, Richard Woodward et al. 1991. _Accounts Overdue: Natural Resource Depreciation in Costa Rica._ Washington, DC: World Resources Institute.

Solow, Robert M. 1974. "The Economics of Resources or the Resources of Economics." _American Economic Review_ (May): 1–13.

————. 1974. "Intergenerational Equity and Exhaustible Resources." _Review of Economic Studies: Symposium on the Economics of Exhaustible Resources_: 29–45.

Toman, Michael A. 1994. "Economics and 'Sustainability': Balancing Trade-offs and Imperatives." Discussion paper (January 1991 revised February 1994). Washington, DC: Resources for the Future.

Toman, Michael A., John Pezzey, and Jeffrey Krautkraemer. 1994. "Neoclassical Economic Growth Theory and 'Sustainability'." ENR 93-14 REV (April). Washington, DC: Resources for the Future.

Wear, David N. 1992. "Forest Management, Institutions, and Ecological Sustainability." Paper presented at Appalachian Society of American Foresters Meeting, at Asheville, NC.

Wilen, James E. 1985. "Bioeconomics of Renewable Resource Use." Pp. 61–124 in _Handbook of Natural Resource and Energy Economics,_ ed. Allen V. Kneese, and James L. Sweeney. Amsterdam: North-Holland.

Chapter 6

To Grasp or Not to Grasp: That Is the Question

> It can be plausibly argued that much of the economic backwardness in the world can be explained by the lack of mutual confidence.
>
> —Kenneth Arrow

The discussion of the previous chapter omitted a crucial variable—human motivation. The ancient Hebrews asserted that we cannot separate economic prosperity, justice, peace, interior maturity, and ecological integrity from one another. By exercising dominion over the earth as the Creator intends, all creation prospers. In other words, the way we as a society approach one another and the rest of creation determines the well-being of us all. Therefore, the way society approaches its garden technically, spatially, and attitudinally affects human welfare, as well as "nature's."

Grasping for control as opposed to trusting and cooperating with others and the Creator makes creation suffer. In chapter 2 we saw that nonhuman creation exhibits strong tendencies toward cooperation. Cooperation aids in survival. Jerusalem understood that when people live out a vision of community in which all seek each others' benefit, all creation enjoys peace and wholeness. Cooperation with humans and the natural processes of creation, "letting go," brings prosperity. However, grasping for control over one's destiny by exploiting the land and its people inevitably destroys the system upon which prosperity ultimately depends, thereby even unmaking creation itself. How does such a worldview relate to the understanding of natural capital, economic

101

growth, and human welfare that we discussed in the last chapter? To understand the connection, as far as we are able, we must explore the relationship of grasping and wisdom to technology, materialism and power, and social capital.

Wisdom and Technology

If ancient Jerusalem could speak to us today, it might charge that our technology represents grasping for control over nature and that grasping lies at the heart of our problems. Our attitudes and culture affect the sorts of problems we perceive and the ways we go about solving them. The search for solutions leads to new technologies for alleviating these problems. The ancient Hebrews believed that receiving the Blessing that sustains the land depends, in part, upon listening to Creation, observing what works, and building upon these insights. Modern technology, however, reflects a desire to conquer nature so that people can obtain what they want from it.[1]

Modern agricultural technology, for instance, involves simplifying ecosystems to large expanses of one (usually hybrid) crop, a monoculture, that is fed artificially high levels of nutrients and, sometimes, artificially high levels of water via irrigation. Herbicides remove other species that attempt to grow as part of the normal process of building plant communities. Other pesticides remove organisms that thrive in the new habitat. By controlling carefully the amount of nutrients, water, and biocides, farmers force certain plants to grow at high rates.

Even without prodding from our ancestors we have come to realize that modern agricultural technology, while very productive, leads to a myriad of environmental problems from loss of soil structure and fertility to poisoned groundwater supplies and pesticide problems. As a result, scientists are examining ecological processes to determine ways to utilize natural forces in the service of humans rather than to work against them. In effect, they are starting to advocate "wisdom," letting go of control and seeking cooperation. Agroecology and "the new forestry" represent fundamental changes in attitude toward agriculture and forestry.

Traditional temperate zone agricultural techniques, when applied in the tropics, often degrade land quickly under the intense heat and rainfall, leading to poverty and further land clearing. Today's agricultural monocultures often provide the farmer with an edge in marketing, mechanization, and other areas. However, monocultures leave farmers vulnerable to price fluctuations, pest outbreaks, and weather. They often tend to deplete natural soil fertility, cause erosion, and increase dependence upon purchased agrochemicals.

By combining modern science with insights from traditional tropical agriculture, agroecology offers hope of finding alternative forms of agriculture that break this cycle.[2] Much of traditional tropical agriculture consists of polyculture, that is, "employing more than one crop—in sequence, combination, or both—and mixing crop and animal production in complex, interrelated units" (Dover and Talbot 1987, p. 32). These farming systems reflect years of cultural evolution, and intimate knowledge of the locale being farmed and the interactions occurring there. Such systems exist because they are well adapted to the areas where they developed. Farmers choose them because they minimize risk and dependence upon purchased inputs, and because they maintain soil quality over time.

Polycultural farming systems vary greatly. One proposed system involves clearing a field and then mimicking forest succession by moving from annuals through successive plantings to an economically valuable mixture of shrubs and trees resembling a natural forest. Java's home gardens resemble this approach. They harness the natural powers of certain plant communities by favoring complementarity rather than endlessly fighting weeds.

Polycultural systems offer many advantages. Utilizing plants of different heights and crown shapes allows maximum exposure to solar energy. Designing mixtures that use deep-rooted plants to pump minerals and water from deeper soil layers and that include legumes that fix atmospheric nitrogen decrease the dependence on expensive manufactured fertilizers. Combining crops may minimize the risk of disease and pest damage. Further, should one crop fail, others may succeed to fill the void, thereby ensuring a resilient agricultural system.

Ewel (1986) points out that while agricultural ecosystems dominated by trees tend to be stable (and therefore low risk), they provide yields that are low compared to those systems using annuals. Consequently, he calls for a shifting landscape mosaic (at least for the tropics) where land utilizing intercropped perennials is interspersed with other parcels planted in agroecosystems at various stages of succession (coffee, bananas, coconuts, fruit, and nut trees). As each patch matures, farmers clear it and start over with a polyculture of annuals. Such a shifting mosaic could offer significant benefits of pest control, low risk, and soil maintenance.

Just as agroecology seeks to cooperate with natural processes in order to create a profitable, sustainable agriculture, so does "the new forestry." Many different approaches fall under this rubric. Natural forest management, for instance, attempts to maintain a highly diverse, but economically profitable forest by silviculturally changing the forest somewhat to promote economically valuable trees. At the same time, forest managers recognize the roles and values of other forest goods and services such as erosion control, healthy and diverse flora and fauna, and financially valuable nontimber products (such as honey, fruits, nuts, and wild game). One simple approach involves marking the largest economically valuable trees for harvest and identifying those trees to be harvested at the next round, for instance, ten years later. Workers clear a relatively small area around trees slated for the next harvest in order to decrease the competition for their nutrients, water, and light, thereby increasing the tree's growth rate. In some areas, oxen haul out the timber, damaging fewer trees and disrupting soil far less than tractors would. New seedlings sprout from seed, or saplings that have been suppressed by the competition for light and nutrients flourish when provided the opportunity afforded by removing the larger trees. Consequently, often natural forest management requires little planting. These techniques maintain a largely natural forest while providing a sustainable source of products at low cost. While natural forest management is still in its early stage of development, its proponents hope that it will prove profitable for firms and small landowners alike.

In the Pacific Northwest of the United States, foresters experiment with alternatives to clear-cutting. Old-growth forests there depend upon downed timber to provide "nursery logs" where seedlings can establish themselves. Standing dead trees provide habitat for owls and other animals. When standard clear-cuts remove much of the downed timber and all standing trunks, they remove much of the natural regeneration capacity of the forest as well as habitat for animals. New forestry techniques emphasize maintaining some mature trees after harvest to provide more tree height variety in a new stand, as well as pruning and selective harvesting to quicken the rate of growth of individual trees. These techniques attempt to re-create the structural characteristics of tree stands that the more mature forests provide.

Scientists promoting "new forestry" also accord far more attention to the interaction of streams and forests and to landscape mosaics. Some now stress maintaining a mosaic of forest stands at different developmental stages in order to provide the diversity a given landscape may require. They also call for interconnected systems of reserved areas and protected zones along streams, along with patches of managed and protected forests of sufficient size to maintain desired ecological characteristics.

These new approaches to agriculture and forestry embody listening, observing, and cooperating, or wisdom. (See chapter 3, where wisdom is discussed.) Thus, ancient tradition may indicate that approaches such as these may be on the right track. It also may indicate that the Amish may have something to say to the rest of us. They select from modern technology only those ''improvements'' that fit within their sense of propriety and culture. In other words, we may wish to consider whether or not we ought to do something just because we can do something.

Materialism and Power

In a similar fashion, just because we may be capable of producing large quantities of goods, does that mean we should? For the Hebrews, personal development requires growing in solidarity with all of creation—seeing ourselves as intimately connected with our surroundings. Solidarity precludes easily accepting environmental degradation in order to obtain more goods. Accumulating goods for their own sake also threatens our relationship with the Creator and others. ''Where your treasure is, there your heart lies.'' Just as Dickens's Scrooge learned that he couldn't love his fiancée (or Bob Cratchit) and money too, we learn the hard way that loving goods more than the Creator and creation leaves little room for relationships and personal growth. By valuing relationships more than goods, Jerusalem's understanding of personal welfare demands less from creation materially than does modern Western thinking.[3]

Our examination of ecosystems showed that limits exist. If ecosystems are disturbed too much, at some time they will ''flip'' to another state. Similarly, if populations exceed their carrying capacity, destruction follows. Yet, modern humanity lives as if it inhabits an ever-expanding garden.

In many ways the materialism that drives a wedge between people and creation represents the beginning of environmental degradation. When we extract more and more resources to satisfy unlimited desires, we place increasing strain on the natural capital stock. An unbalanced, unsustainable capital portfolio is the result. If we curb the desire for material goods by valuing our relationships more than things, we thereby limit the amount of goods any one individual needs for the good life. When we combine this sense of limit with a concern for all of creation, a just distribution of income, and good health and education for all, a much different mix of human, natural, and manufactured capital emerges than in a more materialistic society. Moreover, a society living this way cannot justify sustaining one region, or country, by importing large amounts of energy and matter while degrading exporting regions to do so. It rather would seek to find ways by which all regions could maintain viable communities via a well-balanced combination of natural, human, and manufactured capital.

When people want more and more goods, they also want to control the different stocks of capital in order to be sure they can have more goods. By controlling access to the means of production, whether factories, land, education, food, or health care, individuals and countries determine the amount and distribution of goods, services, power, and status they receive. Control by a few over society's capital portfolio often leads to depreciation of the natural and human capital stock. Guatemala and Appalachia provide good examples.

Guatemala's unjust social structures—the institutionalization of the elite's long history of grasping for control—have degraded her landscapes and threatened her long-run economic viability and well-being. The current inequitable land system began with the king of Spain's granting large tracts of land to the conquistadors. The conquest represented an obvious attempt to control resources for personal and national gain. As a result of this original attempt, nine out of every ten people in present-day rural Guatemala live on plots that are too small, given present farming techniques, to provide the basic needs of a family without outside employment (IBRD 1978). According to 1970 data, 26 percent of rural families have no land while only 2 percent of farm families own 80 percent of Guatemala's agricultural land (IBRD 1978; Weeks 1985, p. 112; cited in Brockett 1988). On the fertile Pacific coastal plain, most of the original rain forest has been converted to cotton, sugar, and other export crops produced by large landowners. Because most of the population lives in the rugged highlands, the population either must migrate out of the highlands or move up the region's steep slopes. This results in high rates of erosion, reduced soil fertility, sedimentation of dam sites, migration to and deforestation of the Petén rain forest, and rapid increases in urbanization. The poverty caused in large part by the lack of access to land stimulates high population growth rates. These, in turn, cause greater pressure on the highlands and further loss of many of the functions formerly performed by the natural systems there and elsewhere. At the same time, the government historically has placed relatively little emphasis on the education and health needs of the rural, largely indigenous population so that human capital formation there remains low. As a result, while manufactured capital formation benefiting the largely urban upper class continues, human capital formation stays low while natural capital depreciates. The growing concern for Guatemala's environment domestically and internationally indicates that the situation indeed is grave.[4]

Farther north in the Clear Fork Valley of Appalachian Tennessee and Kentucky, one company owns 80 percent of the land. This company, the largest landowner on the east coast of the United States, bought the tract from the large British energy conglomerate that originally assembled the acreage around the turn of this century. Local people charge that the original company often obtained the land by a variety of unjust means. Like its predecessor, the current owner leases the land to timber, strip mining, and oil and gas interests but hesitates to make it available to local people for development efforts. Due to the ubiquitous strip mining, the valley has experienced such serious water-quality problems that the U.S. Department of the Interior installed a multimillion dollar centralized water system in an attempt to compensate for the degradation. Employment also suffers as a result of the monopolistic control of land in the area (although typical industrialization and agriculture prove difficult at any rate in this mountainous, isolated area). A grassroots-initiated pallet factory failed, at least in part, due to the company's unwillingness to free its local timber for use as an input for the factory. Importing wood from outside the region proved too expensive. Houses form strip developments (development that occurs only along roadsides) because little acreage is available for homes elsewhere. Sediment from the mines periodically smothers scarce bottomlands, making farming difficult. What few jobs there are exist in the strip mines, so that local people have to ruin their environment to survive (Gaventa 1980, and personal observation). The export of coal sustains electric-power consumers in other areas who benefit at the expense of the local people and the natural systems upon which they depend. The source of the extensive degradation stems from large-scale absentee landownership, the subsequent divorce of land-use decision making from those who live with its impacts, the landowner's apparent lack of concern for all of creation, and the electric consumers' willingness to obtain energy at this region's expense (and/or their ignorance concerning the source of electricity and the ecological consequences of the coal mining that makes it possible).

In both examples, society's institutions embody years of grasping. Land-tenure inequities lead to poverty and pressure on resources either from the large landowners and/or from impoverished residents. The impact that landownership and land use in general have on landscape mosaics, ecological stability and diversity, and the well-being of the human community, largely remains to be studied. In some cases, depending upon the land use, large landholdings may protect the environment. In others, such as those cited here, they lead to degradation and the loss of environmental functions. The scriptural vision linking environmental degradation to institutionalized grasping bears a striking resemblance to liberation theology's politico-theological analysis (also based upon scripture) that views salvation in large part as liberation from institutionalized sin. This vision also resembles political economic dependency theory that sees environmental degradation as resulting from unjust international economic structures. In other words, our interior attitudes get incorporated in institutions that, in turn, affect landscape mosaics. The phenomenon of grasping and the resulting unjust institutional structures often lead to unstable landscape mosaics and impoverished communities.

Grasping and Social Capital

Some of the work in political economy can help us understand how grasping for power becomes institutionalized and self-perpetuating. It also may help clarify the role of competition and of cooperation, a subject we first encountered when studying ecosystems. This section examines these questions. The next chapter applies these insights to the question of how society can achieve both ecological and human well-being.

Neoclassical economics focuses on how the market allocates scarce resources to satisfy various human needs. All societies face the Economic Problem: which goods to produce and how much of each; how much capital, labor, land, and entrepreneurial effort to use in producing each type of good; who should receive the goods produced; where to produce the goods; and how fast the economy should grow (how many resources should be devoted to producing capital goods instead of consumer goods). Neoclassical economics takes as a given the institutions and values of the society, as well as the corresponding distribution of income and wealth of that society. Given any income distribution and the tastes of individuals in the society, the market then efficiently allocates resources to solve the Economic Problem. When the market has done its job, no one can be made better off without someone else being made worse off. Similarly, more of one good cannot be made without society losing some of another good because resources must be drawn from the latter to devote them to the former. Competition assures us that all goods will be produced with as few resources, and costs, as possible. However, given an inequitable distribution of income and wealth, the market will produce an efficient, but inequitable solution. Similarly, a more equal income and wealth distribution probably will result in a more equal sharing of society's goods and services.

Political economy goes beyond neoclassical economics to deal with the fact that all societies must decide who controls resources and who influences policy; that is, society must determine the ownership of resources that constitutes the beginning point for neoclassical economics. Members of society must set the "rules of the game," or institutions, that govern the economic system. These are the legal relationships between individuals and the ways that people expect one another to behave given the preferences all members of society share. Society must determine the nature of property and its legal status, the legal status of workers, and the enforcement of contracts, for instance. It also must determine how neighbors will respond when someone's barn burns or an unincorporated community needs to establish a volunteer fire department. These "rules" provide the arena within which the market allocates scarce resources (Bromley 1993, pp. 3–5).

Machiavelli and others felt that for a society to successfully establish these institutions, its citizens must be full of "civic virtue." They must cherish the broader community and wish to serve it. The later English political theorists such as Hobbes and Locke discredited this view, asserting that only checks and balances within the political system were necessary to provide brakes on rampant individual self-interest. Civic virtue was unnecessary. External checks and balances could replace internal. Over the last twenty-five years, revisionists within U.S. political thought have returned to the importance of civic virtue, drawing inspiration from John Winthrop's admonition to the citizens of his "city set upon a hill": "We must delight in each other, make others' conditions our own, rejoyce together, mourn together, labor and suffer together, always having before our eyes our community as members of the same body" (Putnam 1993, pp. 86–87. Winthrop cited in Putnam, p. 87).

Modern analyses of how individuals organize themselves to take collective action have focused on situations such as the Prisoner's Dilemma and the provision of public goods. Each highlights the problematic aspect of cooperation. Consider open-access resources: beaches where people gather clams whenever they want. These provide an environmental example of the Prisoner's Dilemma.[5] People know that if everyone clams as much as they want, soon no one will have any clams at all. They also realize that if they agree to limit their harvesting, they all will have clams in the future. However, each person knows that, if she or he agrees to the limit, someone else may cheat and harvest even more, leaving her or him with a small harvest. She or he also knows that others may think that *she or he* will cheat, so that they may cheat also. In the absence of some solid reason to trust the others to keep their end of the bargain, everyone ends up furiously clamming in order to get clams before they run out. This leads to the famous "Tragedy of the Commons" that states that the lack of ownership prevalent in open access resources inevitably leads to overexploitation (Hardin 1968). While unfortunate, the individuals act in a rational manner given the likelihood that others will renege on their promise.

As mentioned in chapter 5, public goods consist of those goods with a peculiar characteristic—no one can be excluded from receiving benefits once one person buys (consumes) the good. Consider the fictitious case of Raven's Peak, a large rock pinnacle that towers over the landscape. People come from all over to see this historic landmark, an impressive sight. Jack hopes to protect it from development, so he canvasses his neighbors and visitors for donations to purchase the tract. Each person knows that, once someone has protected the tract, they can enjoy the view for free. So, figuring that someone else will pay, they decline, expecting to get a "free ride" in the future. As a result, Jack receives few donations and soon the Raven's Peak boasts ten hamburger stands and numerous second homes. Getting people to cooperate in providing scenic vistas, or community ambulance services, requires each person's committing to cooperate and not back out at the last minute, hoping to get a free ride.

Followers of Hobbes believe that the answer to the irrationality of cooperation lies in having a third party, the government, enforce cooperation. The government should control access to beaches and scenic vistas by outright ownership or regulation. The government, therefore, provides protection against unbridled self-interest.[6] However, their opponents point out that not only is this solution expensive, but it also is risky—what guarantees that the third party will cooperate for the good of the others and not seek its own self-interest?

Despite the supposed irrationality of cooperation, many cases of cooperative or collective action do exist. The presence of social capital may explain why. Social capital consists of "norms of reciprocity" and of networks of people working together for a common good. Norms, or standards of behavior, cause people to behave in socially desirable ways by socializing them to act accordingly or by providing sanctions that deter undesirable behavior. When someone says they will meet you at the office at 11:00 A.M., if you come from the United States you expect them to arrive there precisely at 11:00 A.M. If they do not, they have reason to expect you to be angry (a sanction) because they broke the norm that people in this society come at the stated hour, not two hours later or tomorrow.

"Generalized reciprocity," another norm, plays a key role in fostering cooperation. Generalized reciprocity consists of doing something for somebody with the expectation that at some time in the future that person will do the same, or some other good thing, in return. It resembles altruism in the short run and self-interest in the long run. Because people expect others to return favors in the future—to reciprocate—they find it easier to extend favors now without expecting immediate reward.

People involved in dense networks of relationships tend to reciprocate. They know that if they do not cooperate when asked, everyone will find out and will extend no favors to them in the future (a sanction). Thus, when my neighbor's barn burns, I help out because, since I have reason to trust him, I reasonably can expect him to help me in the future. The more I help out, the more he will reciprocate, because I have demonstrated my trust in him. The existence of many clubs, civic associations, family groupings, religious organizations, and other civic groups does four things: (1) facilitates the exchange of information on individuals' trustworthiness, (2) increases the cost to individuals of failing to cooperate, (3) fosters mutual trust as the importance of maintaining one's reputation grows, and (4) provides models of successful collaborative ventures (Putnam 1993, pp. 164–73). Civic culture fosters cooperation.

Civic communities, those having what Palmer calls a strong "public life," show the following characteristics. First, people understand that their self-interest includes seeking the common good, so that they actively participate in society. Working together draws individuals out of themselves, creating "other-centeredness." The common, or public, life then becomes more than an opportunity for self-enrichment. This does not imply that people must act altruistically. Rather, civic-minded citizens act out of a self-interest alive to others' interests. Second, members of society strive for political equality. Bonds of reciprocity and cooperation rather than relations of authority and dependency characterize relationships between people. Leaders conceive of themselves as responsible to their community, and are responsible to it. Third, citizens help, respect, and trust one another, and tolerate opponents. They see that mutual aid is both possible and desirable. Fourth, distinctive social practices and institutions embody these norms and values of civic culture. People form varieties of associations to pursue common interests. In these associations people learn that they can overcome conflict and learn how to do it. They come to understand how to take joint action even when they disagree. Citizens overcome their fear of those different from themselves by working together with them on common concerns. Individuals with opposing viewpoints educate one another, moderating and refining their ideas. These voluntary institutions instill habits of cooperation, and attitudes of solidarity and public-spiritedness (Palmer 1981, pp. 40–45; Putnam 1993, p. 87). The more society bears these characteristics, the more "civic" it is.

Putnam's impressive study of regional governments in Italy provides a test of the effect of this "civicness" on a people's ability to work together, as measured by the effectiveness of democratic government. His study also provides insight into the role of civicness on economic development and human satisfaction.

The north and south of Italy differ markedly in their histories and degrees of civicness. The northern part of Italy inherited a strong civic tradition of citizen involvement stemming from the Middle Ages. Southern Italy inherited a feudal system marked by strong patron-client relationships where the powerful members of the community provided assistance and protection for the weaker in return for the latter's loyalty. Whereas northern Italy revolves around interlocking networks of associations and community groups, southern Italy revolves around hierarchical patron-client relationships. One society builds upon trust while the other rests upon fear.

In 1970 Italy established fifteen regional governments with essentially identical constitutional structures and mandates. Putnam asked how well these identical government structures function across the regions that have different civic cultures. Empirical tests of government effectiveness, using a variety of measures, showed strongly that the performance of regional governments could be explained totally by the degree of civicness, even controlling for regional differences in economic development. Moreover, individuals' ratings of their satisfaction with their lives showed that family income, religious observance, and community civicness predicted satisfaction best, with almost equal importance. Although today the most civic regions also are the most economically developed, this did not hold true prior to the turn of the century. Moreover, empirical testing indicates that civic involvement in the early 1900s predicts civicness, government performance, and economic development in the 1980s. Socioeconomic development in the 1900s appears to play no role in explaining these phenomena. While civicness does not account for Italy's development, it does explain why certain regions responded well to the forces leading to growth while others did not (Putnam 1993, pp. 99, 111, 114).[7] Civicness leads to effective government, facilitates modern economic development, and promotes individual happiness.

If the study of Italy serves as a guide for other societies, past generations appear to play an important role in determining the nature of today's society. Institutional patterns tend to reinforce themselves. First, individuals find it easier to adapt to current institutions and norms rather than to try to change them. Second, organizations within society have vested interests in maintaining these institutions and norms and devote much effort to doing so. Third, cooperation or individualistic opportunism become ingrained in the system as organizational learning, cultural habits, and mental models reinforce these behaviors (North 1990 as discussed in Putnam 1993, p. 179). As Gambetta points out,

> Deep distrust is very difficult to invalidate through experience, for either it prevents people from engaging in the appropriate kind of social experiment or, worse, it leads to behaviour which bolsters the validity of distrust itself. . . . Once distrust has set in it soon becomes impossible to know if it was ever in fact justified, for it has the capacity to be *self-fulfilling*. (Gambetta 1988, p. 234, as cited in Putnam, 1993, p. 170)

Virtuous and vicious cycles of behavior, therefore, affect future generations. To paraphrase the Hebrew scriptures, the sins of the forefathers and the blessings of the virtuous are passed down generation upon generation.

Lest we become historical determinists, Putnam points out that changing political structures can make a difference (p. 184). Both the north and south of Italy experienced changing identities, values, power, and strategies as the result of the new regional governments. Both regions' elite political cultures became more moderate, pragmatic, and tolerant as old patterns of power changed. Moreover, the social learning that occurred in the reform process nurtured self-sustaining change. The more civic north, however, experienced more change than did the south.

Other powerful forces, besides political reform, change attitudes and civicness. As we have seen, market forces reward those who choose to defect from cooperative arrangements. Neighbors who together attempt to maintain rural landscapes in the face of rising land prices for urban use or second homes find it increasingly difficult to pass up windfall profits. Once one neighbor sells, other neighbors not only find it more difficult to trust but find that the reason to hold out diminishes as the neighborhood changes character. In other words, the market not only rewards opportunistic behavior but tends to erode trust.[8] The market also erodes relationships by tending to treat land and labor as commodities to be bought and sold rather than relationships to be fostered. When large discount retailers enter a community, they bring a wide variety of products at low prices. However, they may do so at the cost of destroying the network of relationships that existed between the owners and clerks of the local hardware and clothing stores and their customers. The same process, of course, may happen with supermarkets. The labor mobility that moves families from job to job further disrupts community and family relationships. Jeremy Seabrook's interviews, for example, of hundreds of older working-class people in England found them better off economically than their parents, but isolated and unhappy (1978, as cited in Daly and Cobb 1989, p. 163).

Religion, on the other hand, attempts to overcome such brokenness and isolation by bringing reconciliation and forming community. Indeed, the root of the word "religion" means "to rebind" or "bind together." Activity in religious groups, while itself fostering the public life, may not constitute religion's main contribution to civicness. Rather, prayer and contemplation lead one to the Creator, the matrix within which all life exists, thereby creating an awareness of one's connectedness to the Creator and all other life. Paradoxically, strong private spiritual life develops other-centeredness and an interest in public life. Strong public life, in turn, nurtures strong spiritual lives by providing safe, clean, beautiful places to live. The public and spiritual reinforce one another (Palmer 1981, pp. 22–31). It should not be surprising, then, that the Hebrews stressed that the public and spiritual arenas comprise parts of a greater whole. Grasping in one part tends to bring grasping and disorder in the other. Wisdom brings the opposite.

It appears, then, that we can understand, at least in part, the ancients' perspective that motivations play a central role in shaping society and the landscape. Desires to control nonhuman creation and resources create certain types of institutions and technology that affect landscape mosaics and their functions, leading to oppression, poverty, and environmental degradation. Should we be able to analyze at the largest scale, we might find that spiritual forces reinforce these tendencies.

Conversely, human and ecological well-being require other-centered attitudes that include a concern for creation and its integrity and require that humans mirror the cooperation seen in nonhuman creation itself. By learning to cooperate with nonhuman creation and its rhythms and by learning to live for and with others, communities approach the wholeness, or *shalom*, of the Garden. In short, long-term prosperity requires wisdom.

We already have begun to explore what might be necessary to sustain the Garden. The question remains: Given that the market fails in the case of externalities (like dumping pollutants in water), open-access resources (like clams), public goods (like scenic vistas), and landscape patterns (economies of configuration), how can society best organize itself to deal with these problems? What institutional framework that sets the bounds for market activity provides the most likelihood of fostering ecological and human well-being? The next, and final, chapter explores these questions. It examines the roles that changed vision and institutional structures might play in achieving ecologically healthy landscapes, considers the relationships between this goal and sustainable human welfare, and reflects on the differences between standard neoclassical economics and the economics of the Garden.

Notes

1. See, for instance, Austin's (1988) and Mumford's (1970) discussion of modern science and technology, the culture that supports it, and Francis Bacon's contributions to these. Bacon, for instance, believed that science and technology served to extend "the empire of man over things." Humanity manipulates and controls the earth to serve human needs.

2. The following paragraphs on agroecology draw heavily on Dover and Talbot (1987) and Ewell (1986). For discussions of nontropical agroecology see the list of suggested readings.

3. Philip Powell, an economist studying at Vanderbilt University, points out that "residents of Jerusalem" may demand more spiritually than materially from creation. Such demands, however, have no direct ecological impact.

4. Apparently environmentally benign policies can mask grasping. Members of the elite can create parks to satisfy foreign-aid agencies, to provide environmental services the elite desire, or to bring tourist dollars that are spent on businesses the elite control. Establishing the parks, however, can drive subsistence farmers, hunters, and gatherers off the land, increasing poverty and pressure on the remaining unprotected or inadequately managed land resources. Thanks to Philip Powell for this point.

5. The classic, more rigorously defined Prisoner's Dilemma involves two prisoners, Joe and George, awaiting separate interrogations for a crime they jointly committed. Should each refuse to confess, they receive suspended sentences. However, should one confess and the other plead innocence, the one that confesses receives a reward and his freedom while the other goes to jail for years. Should both confess, each receives a short prison sentence. If they trust each other, they both will plead innocent and get off easily. However, Joe knows that if George confesses, Joe will be better off if he confesses too. Should George plead innocence, however, Joe will want to have confessed because by doing so he gains his freedom and a reward, instead of a suspended sentence. Regardless of the action George takes, Joe comes out ahead by confessing. So, he does. Of course, independently George thinks the same way as Joe, and he confesses also. Because both confess, they receive short prison sentences. If they had been allowed to communicate with each other, or if Joe and George had trusted each other to hold tight and had known that the *other* trusted *him* to hold tight, they could have taken the risk of pleading innocence. In the absence of trust, the rational solution, with or without communication, leads to "ratting" on one another (Runge 1981; Ostrom 1990).

6. In dynamic versions of the Prisoner's Dilemma, where the prisoners repeatedly must decide whether or not to confess (e.g., because they face many charges) and they may learn how the other behaves, a cooperative solution tends to emerge. When a prisoner copies the behavior of the other party, cooperating if the other does or confessing if the other does (tit for tat), the game ends with both parties cooperating. This strengthens the argument against the necessity of having a third party to enforce cooperation.

7. For an intriguing discussion of how firms in the decentralized industrial districts in Italy cooperate in providing administration, professional training, information, and other infrastructure and yet compete vigorously with one another, see Putnam 1993, pp. 160–61.

8. See Editors of *The Ecologist* (1993) for a good discussion of the impact of the market on management of common property.

References

Austin, Richard C. 1988. *Beauty of the Lord: Awakening the Senses.* Atlanta: John Knox Press.

Brockett, Charles. 1988. *Land, Power, and Poverty: Agrarian Transformation and Political Conflict in Central America.* Boston: Unwin Hyman.

Bromley, Daniel W. 1993. "Common Property as Metaphor: Systems of Knowledge, Resources, and the Decline of Individualism." *The Common Property Resource Digest* (27): 1–8.

Daly, Herman E., and John B. Cobb, Jr. 1989. *For the Common Good: Redi-*

recting the Economy Toward Community, the Environment, and a Sustainable Future. Boston: Beacon Press.

Dover, Michael, and Lee M. Talbot. 1987. *To Feed the Earth: Agro-Ecology for Sustainable Development*. Washington DC: World Resources Institute.

Editors of *The Ecologist*. 1993. *Whose Common Future? Reclaiming the Commons*. London: Earthscan.

Ewel, John J. 1986. "Designing Agricultural Ecosystems for the Humid Tropics." *Annual Review of Ecology and Systematics* 17: 245–71.

Gambetta, Diego. 1988. "Can We Trust Trust?" Pp. 213–37 in *Trust: Making and Breaking Cooperative Relations*, ed. Diego Gambetta. Oxford: Blackwell.

Gaventa, John. 1980. *Power and Powerlessness: Quiescence and Rebellion in an Appalachian Valley*. Urbana: University of Illinois Press.

Hardin, Garrett. 1968. "The Tragedy of the Commons." *Science* 162 (December 13): 1243–48.

IBRD. 1978. "Guatemala: Economic and Social Position and Prospects." A World Bank Country Study, (August). Washington, D. C.: The International Bank for Reconstruction and Development.

Mumford, Lewis. 1970. *The Pentagon of Power*. New York: Harcourt Brace Jovanovich.

North, Douglass. 1990. *Institutions, Institutional Change, and Economic Performance*. New York: Cambridge University Press.

Ostrom, Elinor. 1990. *Governing the Commons: The Evolution of Institutions for Collective Action*. New York: Cambridge University Press.

Palmer, Parker J. 1981. *The Company of Strangers: Christians and the Renewal of America's Public Life*. New York: Crossroads.

Putnam, Robert D. 1993. *Making Democracy Work: Civic Traditions in Modern Italy*. Princeton: Princeton University Press.

Runge, Carlisle Ford. 1981. "Common Property Externalities: Isolation, Assurance, and Resource Depletion in a Traditional Grazing Context." *American Journal of Agricultural Economics* (63): 595–606.

Seabrook, Jeremy. 1978. *What Went Wrong? Why Hasn't Having More Made People Happier?* New York: Pantheon.

Weeks, John. 1985. *The Economies of Central America*. New York: Holmes & Meier.

Chapter 7

Garden Economics

Thinking of the Garden as a ''common'' can help us understand how humanity can maintain ecologically vital landscapes that nourish communities of life generation after generation. Commons consist of any resource that humans share, as in the case of communal grazing lands or the New England commons. In the broadest sense, humans share in the clams on the beach, scenic vistas, quality of community life, water quality, forests, radio wavelengths, silence, and streets. All these may be considered commons. Some of these goods resemble private goods. When someone consumes a hamburger or a lumber company harvests a tree, for instance, they automatically exclude others from doing so. Other goods more resemble public goods. Everyone enjoys the same radio stations without depleting the amount available to one another. Many commons, such as forest commons, have aspects of both. In this case, one of the outputs of the common, trees, is a private good. Yet, the forest ecosystem, which everyone shares, more closely approximates a public good.

Commons, unless they are managed adequately, share all the problems of externalities, free riders, open-access property, and so forth discussed in chapters 5 and 6 unless they are managed adequately. As seen in chapter 6, humans jointly create their community life, doing well or poorly depending upon their willingness to cooperate. They also jointly create landscape patterns that deliver a certain mix of economic and ecological goods and services. However, because the market fails to account for the personal relationships and economies of configuration, the unaided market can provide neither the ''right'' amount of relationships nor the correct landscape pattern. Institutions other than the market need to deal with the commons.

From the perspective of the Garden, humans should cooperate with one another and creation to manage the commons for two interrelated purposes: (1) to maintain persistent, resilient, and resistant landscapes that preserve as many species as possible and that maintain future options for society, and (2) to foster human well-being, or development. Let us first consider the land-management systems that humans use and consider what system(s) might best achieve the first of these two goals. Then we will consider how that system might affect human well-being.

DIM Structures

All land-management systems contain decision-making, information, and motivation (DIM) structures, which are closely interrelated.[1] The decision-making structure established by society determines who has authority over various land and resource decisions and what the basis for that authority is. For instance, individuals, communities, the state, or no one at all may exercise decisions on how to use land or certain parcels of land. The authority to make decisions may stem from private or communal property rights, tradition, or claims of national patrimony. The information structure includes the means for gathering, transmitting, accumulating, retrieving, processing, and analyzing information on the impacts of various land-management practices. It also transmits information on the actual or contemplated actions of the various actors making decisions about land and of the impacts of such actions. The motivation structure deals with how decision makers wield their authority. It consists of the goals of the various decision makers and how one decision maker may attempt to motivate another to act as he wishes. Should these three structures fail to mesh adequately, then the entire land-management process loses effectiveness.

Consider the decision-making structure of the private ownership system in developed and some Third World countries. In this system the landowner has the authority to use the land as she sees fit, subject to any legal restrictions the state may impose. Thus, the authority lies in both the individual and state to varying degrees depending upon the locale. The state can affect individual land-management decisions by adding to or eliminating options or by influencing perceived options; for example, by building a hydroelectric reservoir next to the property, providing agricultural and forestry extension services, restricting land to certain uses (zoning), raising interest rates or subsidizing tractors, or raising fears or expectations of any of these actions. Alternatively, society may affect the consequences of a decision maker's acts or his perceptions of those consequences, for instance by imposing fines for allowing sediment to enter a stream or threatening to fine those who fail to mow their grass. Finally, society may change landowners' preferences and thereby change their practices. Environmental education may serve such a function, as when the landowner on the Osa Peninsula "saw the light" and decided to reforest rather than cut down more trees (see the last section of chapter 5).

The information and motivation systems of the private-ownership system faces particular difficulties in the face of problems such as externalities, environmental public goods, and economies of configuration (see chapters 5 and 6). When combined with unclear property rights, insecure access to land (tenure problems), and conflicting and/or inappropriate government policies, the systems often fail. When owners live on their land, over time they learn how it responds to various management techniques. Indeed, their culture may have accumulated and tested knowledge over time.[2] However, they often lack scientific information with which to improve traditional techniques. They also may lack information on the impacts that others' land-management decisions have on their land. When economic or social well-being does not depend directly upon the way the land is treated, owners may lack the motivation to treat it well unless they wish to do so on moral grounds. In addition, when many owners make decisions in a region, the market may fail to coordinate their decisions. Not only do owners have a hard time knowing who they are affecting and who is affecting them, and how much, but the costs of finding this out, informing all parties, and organizing them to take action may exceed the benefit to any one individual who may wish to provide leadership—a public goods problem. While the state could serve this function, it often lacks the sufficiently detailed and accurate knowledge about the conditions in every locale of its jurisdiction with which to formulate policy that accounts for externalities or economies of configuration. "Broad-brush" policies intended to promote environmental values over a whole country may not fit well with the contemporary reality of certain locales, and may prove ineffective or deleterious. Some policies may seem particularly onerous to landowners, which may lead to resentment and attempts to circumvent or change the policies. In other cases, especially in the Third World, government may lack the resources and ability to establish appropriate and enforceable land policies.

State and private absentee (particularly large business) ownership of land have their own DIM shortcomings that stem from management decisions being made at a distance. Because state officials and corporate managers who make land-use decisions often live far from the areas they supervise, they typically lack sufficiently accurate and timely information about the impacts of their decisions. Information must pass from on-site managers up through the bureaucracy. This process takes time and distorts information. Managers and/or their institutions often lack a long memory of changes on the land and of the impacts of their activities. They chronically have difficulty in distinguishing between short- and long-term processes. Accordingly, they often do the wrong things, do too little to avert unfavorable impacts of their decisions, and act too late.

Management at a distance also creates motivation problems. Wealthy individuals or corporation managers may not care about their management impacts because they do not reside on the land (and therefore do not personally bear the brunt of their and others' management decisions), and because any negative impacts may have negligible impacts on their balance sheet or social status.[3] Managers at many levels may lack the motivation to treat land in an environmentally sound manner because they may be rewarded for political loyalty, for justifying more staff and budget, and for production of timber or other resources instead of ecologically sound management. They may fail to take action on environmental problems on the grounds that it is not their responsibility. On-site managers may lack authority to make decisions, lack strong interests in the land (because they move frequently and may take an "it's only a job" attitude), and receive little encouragement for taking initiative or trying new approaches. Finally, managers' unquestioned adherence to capitalism, socialism, or other ideologies (including environmentalism!) may prevent them from noticing, or paying attention to, particular ecological details or problems.[4]

These bureaucratic (administered) systems may deal well with problems that are familiar, routine, and static, and may mobilize resources quickly and effectively to reach unambiguous, tangible goals. However, many ecological problems related to land management can be characterized best by their uncertainty, complexity, indivisibility (inability to be broken down into components that can be attacked effectively in isolation), and variability across time and space—the antithesis of routine, static problems. Accordingly, bureaucratic systems tend to fail because of information and motivation problems (Dryzek 1987, pp. 28–29, 108).

Apart from their DIM structures, the failure of relatively complex societies to manage land ecologically stems from perceptual problems. Social change often diminishes a people's perception of their interrelatedness with creation. This leads to environmental degradation and confused priorities. In Bernstein's (1981) view, ecological anthropology provides many examples of how the incorporation of isolated cultural units into larger economic and political structures changes decision-making criteria from those including feedback about environmental effects to those that do not. Incorporating people into larger social structures also tends to drive a wedge between individual perceptions of self-interest and ecological feedbacks that affect individuals' well-being. The concern for immediate consumption then overrides empirical information on the long-term, detrimental effects of the consequences of their actions. Such changes occur easily when humanity's use of the environment grows faster than the rate at which individuals can assimilate information about the negative consequences of their actions. For instance, villagers easily perceive the effects of crop rotations on their yields and respond quickly to this information. However, electricity consumers may not even think to ask whether a relationship exists between their energy use and acidified lakes hundreds of miles from the distant power plants whose emissions *may* have caused the problem.

In his comprehensive review of anthropological theory on the relationship between humans and the rest of creation, Bennett (1975, cited in Bernstein 1981) concludes that throughout history, societies undergo "the ecological transition." As societies pass through this transition, they experience an ever-increasing awareness of their interrelations with other human systems (societies) but a decreasing awareness of their interrelations with nonhuman systems. For instance, whereas in years past we barely knew Ethiopia existed but knew the farmer who grew our tomatoes, now we see reports of famine in Ethiopia and Bangladesh on CNN but don't know where the food on our dinner table comes from. The ecological transition threatens the foundations of human survival by changing our perceptions of our relationship with creation, and thereby affecting our perceptions of self-interest and our subsequent decision making.[5]

Gardening the Common

Given the above difficulties, how might societies move toward more ecologically sound institutional structures for land management?

Restructuring mental maps

Where people possess exploitative, nonrelational, and unecologically sound attitudes toward land, they first need to learn new ways of seeing the earth and new ways they could behave. In *The Structure of Magic*, Bandler and Grinder demonstrate that people act according to their perceptions of the way the world works—their mental maps of the world. People's languages influence the way they see the world by providing categories for organizing information and biasing the interpretation of that data (Bandler and Grinder 1975, chap. 1).[6] Similarly, Tversky and Kahneman (1981) demonstrate that the way a problem is framed, or presented, affects the way that decision makers evaluate outcomes and their probabilities, thereby affecting their preferences. Erikson (1963, 1968; cited in Bernstein 1981, p. 325) shows that individuals can change their perceptual frames to include or exclude certain types of information. One's perceived self-interest, therefore, depends upon the model of the world one lives in.

Behavior changes when people learn to perceive the world differently. When, because of their mental maps, they believe that only certain types of options are open to them, they act rationally according to their perception of reality. However, by changing the social and individual "filters" with which they interpret their experiences and construct their model of reality, people can learn that other options for behavior exist of which they were unaware. Their rational behavior then may change, given that their world has changed (Bandler and Grinder 1975, chap. 1). If we are to begin to garden, to manage our land ecologically, we must restructure our perceptions of the world to include our interrelationships with all the parts of our environment, human and nonhuman.[7] This requires us to rethink our values, lifestyles, relationships, and goals.

Society can aid this process further by allowing different mental maps to be played out on the landscape. By allowing different approaches to land management to be implemented and tested, and widely disseminating the results of these social and technological experiments, people's perceptions of what works and does not work can be challenged by new and old ways of relating to the earth (Hess 1992). Because of the tremendous ecological and economic uncertainty involved in land management, the lack of knowledge of the biophysical systems and of ecological impacts of different ways of using the land, we may expect the process to involve a great deal of trial and error (Ostrom 1990, p. 33). Policymaking under these conditions must allow for experimentation. Should citizens or policymakers want to know the solution in advance, and refuse to act until all information is known, they may paralyze the policy process. Alternatively, policymakers and constituents faced by complex problems may settle for simplistic, less-realistic approaches. Either approach fails to address the complexity of land-management issues.

Building social capital

Restructuring mental maps to be more ecologically sound will not by itself, however, bring ecologically sound land management. Firey (1963), for instance, realized that beliefs or values by themselves do not motivate people to act in a manner consistent with them. He asked why U.S. farmers consistently espoused a conservation ethic but often failed to act on it. Firey felt that people need to believe that conservation is morally correct in order to engage in it. In addition, he hypothesized that conservation values must be embedded within social relationships in such a way that farmers realize they probably will have to conserve anyway (due to community pressures or sanctions) and that conservation benefits the community as a whole. Values that no longer are perceived as critical to community survival will tend to lose control over behavior over time and die out. Thus, values must be embedded in institutions to be effective.[8]

As seen in chapter 6, norms, one social institution, play a crucial role in determining behavior. Many of the ways being explored today for overcoming the DIM problems discussed above involve bringing landowners and/or managers together in various cooperative arrangements. Networks of voluntary associations foster the norms of cooperation essential to such arrangements. By bringing people together over community concerns, including land issues, people not only revise their perceptions about one another and creation but build social capital. The new norms that emerge from these interactions tend to institutionalize new ways of seeing things. For instance, consider a community cleanup and environmental education effort. If the effort has worked well, not only will people express the opinion that dumping garbage is unacceptable, but they also may ostracize those that do it, providing waste cans and garbage collection options as alternatives. To the extent that the community succeeds in internalizing and communicating the sense that garbage-dumping hurts the community, and to the extent that people have come to value the community itself, community members most likely will dump garbage far less frequently than before.

Strong norms of behavior can cause individuals to not even consider some options perceived as wrong, or to perceive a very high cost to doing them. Or, I may decide it is not worth the opprobrium of my neighbors to do it. Norms put a fence around the market, determining when and where market forces are acceptable and unacceptable.[9] Should people come to care enough and know enough about how products are made, they may stop demanding them. Alternatively, people may deem buying such products so unacceptable that buyers may stop buying because of the social cost of doing so. This norm could be institutionalized in laws, regulations, or steep taxes on these products. By removing the profitability of environmentally unsound behavior, due to lack of demand or large sanctions, the market would move elsewhere. Strong norms and strong community relationships also lower the cost of finding violators and punishing them. Accordingly, these norms frame individuals' understanding of self-interest.

Developing new structures

New DIM structures must generate information of the type useful to addressing the uncertainty of ecological issues. Because mental maps condition the way people see ecological issues, an information system must be able to break through established ways of seeing and get information to people who will act upon it. Such a system would have the following five characteristics: (1) all the important stakeholders (people/groups with an interest in the outcome of some issue) would be involved; (2) all participants would possess equal decision-making power and information; (3) all would share a common arena for communicating with one another; (4) their communications would be organized around a common task; and (5) all participants would bring experience to this task.[10] By focusing on the assumptions and interests of the stakeholders, the system would seek to develop group learning and those transformations of perspective necessary to achieving a solution satisfactory to everyone. Such a learning process would be long and arduous, and therefore justified only where the task were controversial, important, and difficult to handle by other, more traditional means (Innes 1990, p. 39). Land management, particularly on larger scales, often meets these criteria.

Local people represent one important group all too often omitted from environmental and land-management decision making. For several reasons they typically will need to be actively involved in land-management decisions affecting their region. First, they often may possess substantial ecological knowledge that they and other interested parties can use to manage land effectively. When people have lived on the land for long periods of time, this particularly will hold true. Where migrants have recently entered the area or elders have failed to pass ecological knowledge on to younger generations, local residents will have less to offer (Gottfried, Wear, and Lee 1994, p. 11). Second, they quickly receive feedback on the impacts of land management. Third, they may depend greatly on the ecological health of the land and, therefore, possess the motivation to manage it well.

Their involvement may prove critical in the Third World. In their review of Third World development efforts, Esman and Uphoff (1984, pp. 40, 99–180, in Putnam 1993, pp. 90–91) concluded that these networks were essential to overcoming mass poverty in Third World-type settings. Moreover, they noted that the most successful grassroots organizations consisted of initiatives begun by local people from relatively cohesive communities. Grassroots initiatives instigated from the outside had higher failure rates. The economic development literature increasingly stresses the importance of grassroots efforts and those of nongovernmental organizations.

A study of thirty World Bank projects from the 1970s found that those projects deemed ''culturally appropriate'' had a rate of return of 18 percent compared to 9 percent for others. Local involvement helped assure that projects were culturally acceptable. Similarly, a study of fifty-two U.S. Agency for International Development projects found a strong correlation between local participation and project success, particularly when locals created and managed their own participatory process (IBRD 1992, p. 94). Grassroots organizations have shown an ability to deal with problems of concern to the people themselves by harnessing local creativity, energy, and knowledge; creating innovative social structures to address local issues; and raising the probability that prospective beneficiaries of development efforts actually will receive benefits from those efforts. When provided with an institutional framework that supports grassroots initiatives, they can achieve a great deal.[11]

Alternative Institutional Approaches to Land Management

As values themselves change and new norms and DIM structures institutionalize these new values, what sorts of structures would overcome best the shortcomings of the present systems? Would these new approaches tend to emphasize cooperation (the Garden's approach) or coercion (the Hobbesian approach)? As it turns out, many of the institutional alternatives being discussed and implemented today involve grassroots efforts and cooperation among the various people considered with the land. The following sections examine three main approaches, all cooperative in focus: common-property regimes, quasi-CPR proposals, and broad-based cooperative approaches.

Common-property regimes

Common-property regimes (CPRs) have existed for centuries in many parts of the world and have succeeded admirably in sustainably managing resources. CPRs consist of commons where the community has regulated the manner by which individuals may appropriate, or harvest, the produce of the commons. Unlike open-access property, where no one manages jointly used resources (i.e., whales, clams on public beaches), in CPRs communities manage the resource that all members share jointly. They manage their commons.

The CPRs share characteristics of public and private goods. While the resource itself (e.g. grazing land) is a public good, the output (the hay) is a private good. Should users appropriate too much hay by overgrazing, the pasture may become unusable—the tragedy of the commons. Because the cattle owners rely heavily on the pasture for their livelihood, they have the motivation to manage it sustainably. Consequently, they devote a lot of energy over the years in a process of trial and error until they discover some system that successfully enables them to regulate themselves.

Consider the case of CPRs in Japan. Forests and uncultivated mountain plains currently cover about two-thirds of Japan. Of this area, rural villages held about one-half as common land as of 1867. At this time of the Meiji restoration, much of this land was redesignated or sold as private or public property. However, 2.5 million hectares of common land still remain in Japan today. Classic CPRs in Japan deal with the harvesting of natural products such as thatch for roofs, fodder, firewood, wood for various purposes, and medicinal herbs. Only individuals, households, or members of the village CPR can harvest. They often do so at designated times according to certain rules developed by the village itself. Other CPRs prohibit use of the commons by individuals and use the proceeds of harvest to supplement village income, distributing it among the coowners or reinvesting it in the commons. In other cases, the village divides the commons into parcels that individuals then use, subject to the restrictions that they may not sell the land and must abide by certain rules of use. Villages that no longer possess sufficient labor to maintain the common lease the land to others who then utilize the resources (McKean 1992, pp. 64–66).

Ostrom (1990, chap. 2) hypothesizes that individuals decide to participate in CPRs according to a cost-benefit-type calculation. She points out that organizing users of a common property is an uncertain and complex undertaking, especially given the unpredictability of "nature," the lack of knowledge about the biophysical system, and the impacts of human disturbance. People tend to value the future less than the present; that is, they discount benefits and costs. The rate at which they discount future benefits depends upon several factors: the likelihood that they will be using the resource in the future, the degree of economic security they possess (the less secure they are the more they will stress present benefits), the probability that others will destroy the resource, and general community norms regarding the present and the future. Communities with stable, economically secure populations tend to work together more to manage their resources than those with unstable, insecure populations. Similarly, communities whose members depend upon the resource for their livelihood, possess few possibilities for securing income outside of their area, and expect one another to cooperate, tend to work together more to manage the common resource than do communities lacking these characteristics.[12]

The relative fairness of these CPRs tends to reinforce cooperation. Private property regimes undergoing population growth either tend to exclude individuals via primogeniture[13] or divide parcels into smaller, and ultimately, more uneconomic parcels. CPRs, on the other hand, tend to exclude no members when faced with population growth. Rather, they often attempt to provide alternative means of income to their young. Moreover, elites find it difficult to render another member entirely powerless (Runge 1981, pp. 29, 31; Bromley 1992, pp. 12–13; Editors of *The Ecologist* 1993, p. 18).

In her study of CPRs throughout the world, Ostrom (1990) found that all the more complex, enduring CPRs she studied used multiple layers of nested enterprises. Irrigation systems provide good examples. For instance, farmers who irrigate land in the region around Valencia, Spain, organize their irrigation system on three to four levels that, in turn, are nested in local, regional, and national governmental jurisdictions. The problems facing farmers obtaining water from secondary canals differ from those on tertiary canals. Establishing uniform rules for irrigators regardless of location would cause confusion. By having several groupings, so that each could develop its own rules on how and when to use water, the entire system can function well over long periods of time. Similarly, because the problems of user groups differ from those of managing the entire system, the Philippine federation of irrigation systems uses two levels of organization, one for local users and one for the overall system.

In many ways it makes sense to promote the CPR approach, particularly in Third World settings. First, many citizens of Third World countries already depend upon them. Promoting CPRs directly helps the most disadvantaged sectors of Third World society (IBRD 1992, p. 142).[14] Second, poverty eliminates many other options for institutional arrangements. Well-defined and enforced private property systems may cost too much for poor societies to run effectively, making joint-use rights (CPRs) a necessity. Third, CPRs provide access to natural resources, the main source of livelihood for many poor people. Private-property systems often lead to inequitable distributions of land and resources, as we have seen earlier; CPRs help prevent this from happening. Fourth, given the uncertainties of weather and crop prices, CPRs provide a form of insurance against individual crop failures and death. Everyone shares in the bounty of the resource so that one does not starve while others feast. They, of course, also share the risk of crop failures (Runge 1992, pp. 19–20). Finally, CPRs address the DIM pathologies prevalent in modern societies.

CPRs do offer drawbacks, however. Population growth, technological change, increased employment opportunities, government interference, lack of credit, changes in the power base of local elites, and envy of outside cultures all can weaken the cohesiveness of the relationships and norms that hold CPRs together, leading to their collapse and subsequent environmental degradation. Community-based approaches may work better in community-oriented cultures, such as those of Asia and the Pacific Islands. In other cultures the distribution of power or struggles for power within the community may jeopardize effective community-resource management.[15] Where CPRs have failed due to changes in society, it may cost a lot to rehabilitate or reinstitute them. Whether the costs outweigh the benefits is difficult to say, particularly in some Third World settings where few other options may exist. Finally, relying on CPRs requires not only national political support, but also "political entrepreneurs" who can engender the trust of local people and demonstrate the tangible benefits of cooperative management. Particularly in Third World countries such individuals can be scarce (IBRD 1992, pp. 95–96, 142–43; Editors of *The Ecologist* 1993, p. 20).

CPRs offer much to First World countries, also. In many ways, the Nature Conservancy, and hunting and golf clubs represent forms of community management of a resource.[16] By overcoming the information and motivation pathologies inherent in bureaucratic systems and by providing the potential for accounting for externalities, public goods, and economies of configuration, CPRs offer the possibility of establishing institutions that enable the market to operate more optimally.

Quasi-CPR proposals

In a proposal that closely resembles CPRs, Dryzek (1987) calls for a radical decentralization of land management. Local communities would manage their own land through a process of "practical reason." Practical reason engages the members of a community in examining both their valued goals and the means used to attain them. Communities would determine their own values and approaches to land management through participatory, discursive, collective problem solving. For example, by placing management of waste disposal in the hands of local communities that rely on their own land and water resources, local communities would allow waste disposal only to the extent they judge appropriate. This would prevent outside influences from exploiting or polluting local resources without local consent. Local communities must pay attention to negative environmental feedback from their management decisions. Feedback travels quickly and more accurately to them than to distant decision makers.

Dryzek sees the greatest difficulty in coordinating communities. Local communities might send representatives to regional groups that, in turn, would be represented at the national level. However, Dryzek suspects that either these groups would deadlock or that the consensual decision making he envisions on the local level would deteriorate into administrative or bargaining modes of decision making.[17] He feels more confident that practical reasoning fora could address specific issues. He describes a forum organized around the siting of oil and gas pipelines from Canadian Arctic sources to city markets. It included all parties interested in the issue. Practical reasoning methods enabled the members of the forum to reach consensus (p. 237).

Because the federal government has owned so much land in the western United States and has espoused basically one (flawed) vision for landscape management, Hess (1992) believes that the federal government has caused much of the environmental degradation in the west. By dispersing ownership among many different groups, no one group's inadequate mental maps and management practices would have the capacity to degrade such large tracts of land. Over the course of twenty years, Hess would have the government grant one hundred shares of all Bureau of Land Management (BLM) and U.S. Forest Service (USFS) land in the western United States to every U.S. citizen holding a Social Security number. Anyone, except national or state government, could purchase these shares from individuals not wishing to maintain ownership. According to Hess, this process should lead to much western land being held by communities and citizen associations. Single individuals and large firms would lack the resources or interest to acquire those lands considered most desirable for recreation, wildlife, and wilderness. Those lands, ostensibly, would have the least potential for logging and/ or grazing.

Hess's approach would create a mosaic of decentralized commons managed according to different visions of what the landscape should be, with owners (individuals or community) bearing the cost and receiving the benefits of their management practices. Having many competing visions operating on the landscape would permit a comparison of their viability—a "market of visions." Hess does not appear to deal with economies of configuration, coordination between communities at the watershed or landscape scale, the availability of social capital, or questions of information generation. While it is a thought-provoking analysis and proposal, his approach may require some modification and more thought.

Broad-based cooperative approaches

The Pacific Rivers Council offers a proposal for large-scale land management that builds upon cooperative institutions already used widely in the United States. The council successfully spearheaded the effort to push the Oregon Omnibus National Wild and Scenic Rivers Act, the largest river protection act in the lower forty-eight states, through the U.S. Congress (Doppelt et al. 1993). Yet, in attempting to develop effective river-management plans for these rivers, the council encountered two problems that derailed their efforts. First, they met stiff private-landowner opposition, Second, the USFS and BLM lacked effective policies to protect tributaries in headwaters or areas outside of the corridors designated by the act. As a result the council worked for two years with conservation groups, scientists, public agencies, and others to develop new policy proposals to overcome these obstacles. The council then made the following proposal for restoring the riverways of the United States.

The council proposed using watersheds as the basic unit of management. Watersheds comprise all those lands drained by a given stream system. The council viewed watersheds as a mosaic of terrestrial-habitat patches drained by a stream network that is a mosaic of aquatic-habitat patches. Because human activities can fragment and disconnect patches, the council stated that watershed management must consider the entire landscape mosaic. Because the headwaters largely control the quality of downstream water, management must focus on these areas as well as other critical patches that provide aquatic refuges for at-risk species or that play critical roles in the functioning of the stream. Of course, the same concept can be applied to the terrestrial landscape. The council's approach emphasized targeting efforts to prevent further degradation, and then later restoring degraded areas.

To accomplish the above, the council recommends a bottom-up, grassroots approach that empowers local communities, alters federal-state-local government roles, and forges links between local people and other interest groups. Where multiple ownerships and political jurisdictions occur in the watershed (i.e., where the watershed does not lie only on federal lands) "watershed councils" play a key role. These nonprofit organizations include "key private landowners, residents, citizen organizations, concerned citizens, and river advocates" (p. 106). Elected government officials at all levels and government agencies either may participate in the council or serve as advisors. These councils are widely used in the East and Upper Midwest. More and more now are emerging in the West, particularly in the Pacific Northwest. Watershed councils not only develop and implement watershed restoration plans but also coordinate management policies along the river. In addition, they may take the responsibility for developing new jobs in river restoration that can revitalize the local community.

Of course, this cooperative approach requires a supportive environment. It requires sufficient technical and financial resources to provide independent scientific assessments of the condition of the watershed and of the measures needed to restore it. All interested parties would receive this information in this approach. The system would build in long-term monitoring and accountability, so that it would be clear whether or not people were achieving their goals. This grassroots approach includes educating the public about the river and their relationship to it. Federal and state governments would stop playing their predominant roles of regulator and enforcer and instead would emphasize:

1. providing locally tailored incentives for landowner participation, as well as incentives to foster the participation of marginalized, disadvantaged groups and river-oriented groups
2. providing a legislative framework so that bottom-up policies and programs would have the force of law
3. requiring that public agencies act in a manner consistent with restoration goals
4. assuring landowners that participation in the process would not

lead to government control or lost economic opportunities (Doppelt et al. 1993, pp. 65–69).[18]

The council's approach bears a striking resemblance to the information system recommended above for dealing with complex, uncertain ecological issues (see the discussion on DIM). It mirrors the CPR approach, but brings together a broader community of all stakeholders, including nonresidents. On large landscapes the councils could work together at another level to deal with economies of configuration. By bringing together different, often conflicting parties, the approach offers the opportunity for reconciliation and consensus-building that enables the problems of public goods, externalities, and open-access property to be addressed. In short, it may provide another form of CPR. For these councils to operate effectively, however, the participants must develop sufficient trust that they can overcome the problems stemming from perceived or actual opportunistic behavior.

These councils resemble the environmental partnerships that are forming between different groups in society. Long and Arnold (1995) define environmental partnerships as "voluntary, jointly-defined activities and decision-making processes among corporate, non-profit and agency organizations that aim to improve environmental quality or natural resource utilization" (p. 10). While broader in scope than land use, some deal directly with land-management issues. For instance, in Oregon a conservation group, 1000 Friends of Oregon, and the Homebuilders Association of Metropolitan Portland (HBAMP) jointly drafted, revised, and promoted the adoption of city and county comprehensive land-use plans. The conservation group realized that their goal of preserving rural land required carefully planned, denser urban development. By working with HBAMP, 1000 Friends obtained that type of development while HBAMP gained increased opportunities for housing construction, shorter permit processes, and less-restrictive zoning practices (Long and Arnold 1995, section 4.5).[19]

As usual, cooperation emerges best in certain environments. Four conditions appear to promote the formation of environmental partnerships: (1) reaching thresholds that threaten irreversible environmental change, as in the cases of the Chesapeake Bay and the Everglades; (2) broad public interest, as when community groups fight industrial polluters; (3) threatened or existing environmental regulation; and (4) clearly identified opportunities for all sides in an environmental issue to win (Long and Arnold 1995, pp. 41–42). Given these conditions, three additional factors appear to contribute to the success of partnerships. Once again, the quality of the relationships that occur among the participants and organizations determines success, as does the presence of dynamic leaders who see the opportunity for cooperation and act upon it. Second, participants' goals must relate to visions of resource conservation or environmental quality. Otherwise, partnerships represent only tactical means for achieving the more narrowly defined interests of the organizations. Finally, partnerships must be able to build the capacity to engage nonparticipants, obtain resources, and create mechanisms so that their agreements result in tangible environmental results.

The erosion of social capital hampers building partnerships. When environmental disputes have engendered deep hostilities, distrust, and misconceptions among groups, as in the case of the spotted owl/old-growth forest controversy in the northwestern United States, it may prove exceedingly difficult for participants to trust one another sufficiently to begin any form of cooperation. Various sides on U.S. environmental issues also know how to use the political system to their advantage. They may give up confrontational tactics only reluctantly in favor of a less-proven approach. The lack of ecological knowledge and number of highly diverse, active, and empowered stakeholders make the establishment of environmental partnerships a challenging prospect (Long and Arnold 1995, pp. 47–48). Yet, more and more partnerships are emerging.

The best structures

Interestingly, all the approaches discussed above stress cooperative action and community life to some degree. The cooperative approach indicated by the Garden appears viable in general. The structures, however, differ substantially in the types of actors involved and the roles allowed individuals, interest groups, states, and firms. Given the complexity and variety of natural and social systems, the capacity to act, and the resources available to people and institutions throughout the world, we can expect no one approach to be the answer. The Hebrew scriptures stress the need for justice and strong, self-giving relationships between creation and the Creator. The precise form that institutions should take falls more in the category of wisdom—learning what works within given contexts and time periods.

Certainly, the degree of complexity societies face recommends substantial flexibility and experimentation. Societies that can allow a variety of approaches and learn from their successes and failures probably will succeed more quickly and thoroughly in sustainably managing land than societies without this capacity.

While Garden economics stresses cooperative approaches to land management, this does not imply that the state need play no role. As discussed earlier, the state must provide a supportive environment for these institutions. The state can focus on facilitating the formation of CPRs, councils, and partnerships, providing technical assistance and funding, and promoting ecological research aimed at improving management. Because of the value of building social capital, and because of the importance to human welfare of building trusting relationships (see below), the state may decide that building social capital through building cooperative land-management institutions may warrant the effort even when social capital is low.[20]

Hess points out that people only need secure control over their landscapes, not necessarily traditional "ownership" (1992). Where the state owns land, peaceful means exist to transfer control from state to private hands. It should be possible, therefore, for state lands to be managed by community groups or broader cooperative organizations that are held accountable for their environmental stewardship. Or, the state could turn over ownership and control of its lands to cooperative groups with certain restrictions or oversight, if necessary. The state also could focus its ownership and/or acquisition of lands in areas critical to providing ecological goods and services and ecological vitality, working with other groups managing surrounding areas.

Where the state owns land and has the resources to devote to its management, *and where social capital is low and difficult to build*, the state may need to play an active management role. However, it may find that it, too, should experiment with different institutional and technical approaches. Giving personnel substantial authority for decision making, having them live for long periods of time in the areas they manage, and making them directly accountable for ecological results may improve the state's effectiveness. These represent movements in the direction of forging stronger relationships between people and land and of developing individuals (see below). Encouraging managers to work with groups interested in the land may help also, particularly when state lands represent only a portion of the landscape that require management.[21]

Where the state has few resources, once again CPRs and some other cooperative arrangements may prove more effective than attempts at state control. The state can seek assistance from nongovernmental organizations and international agencies in formulating adequate legal and policy frameworks and providing the necessary support for such efforts. Some of the above approaches may imply redefining and/or redistributing property rights, land reforms of various types, and political reforms. It should not surprise us that such complex socioecological problems may require society to change in order to address them. The willingness of society to consider such change may serve as a measure of its awareness of and concern about economic and ecological sustainability.

Should society depend to some degree on local groups to manage land, it may need to address the effects of national and international economic forces on landscape management. As we have seen in previous chapters, market forces exert much influence on landscape pattern. Highly competitive markets with many buyers and sellers (ones that economists call perfectly competitive) excel in providing consumers with goods and services at the lowest possible cost—they excel in efficiency. However, they have no mechanisms to assure that society receives the amount of equity (as in the form of the distribution of income), community, or landscape patterns that society desires. Markets cannot provide the proper amount of public goods such as these.[22] Therefore, society may have to decide whether or not the current institutional frameworks within which the market functions provide the human and ecological well-being it desires.

For instance, can large corporations, whether national or multinational, with no ties to particular locations adequately take into account the needs of local communities and landscapes? Their distant managements and anonymous owners usually do not care, for instance, when their decisions to move plants from one location to another disrupt community life and ecological processes. Although cases certainly exist where large corporations have taken such concerns into account, the incentive structure of the market generally promotes ignoring these values and promotes single-minded pursuit of profit. Other organizational structures, such as employee-owned or controlled firms, may promote taking into account local concerns more than traditional structures.[23]

Such considerations also lead one to ask whether or not unfettered international free trade necessarily leads to sustainable landscapes and strong communities. The argument for free trade rests on maximizing the efficiency of the global economy, not on providing sustainable welfare for people. While efficiency certainly promotes the provision of more goods and services, people's well-being also depends upon how those goods and services get distributed among the populace and what happens to its landscapes and communities. Producing goods more efficiently may lead to losses in distributional equity, communities, and landscapes. Therefore, society may have to develop a more nuanced approach to trade that balances gains in efficiency against losses in other values. Economics studies the problem of trade-offs—the costs that all changes or activities incur. Economists would do well to examine the social and ecological trade-offs involved in free trade so that societies could have a better theoretical apparatus with which to approach international trade negotiations and commercial policies.[24]

Gardening and Sustainable Development

> . . . [R]eform and development efforts will not achieve their aims if they are not also suffused with an ecological ethic that recognizes the conjugal bond between humankind and the natural world from which there can be no divorce.
>
> —E. P. Eckholm, *Losing Ground*

The effort to create sustainable landscapes fosters human development. As we noted in chapters 3 and 4, the ancient Hebrews saw the world in terms of a three-way covenant between Creator, humans, and the land (nonhuman creation). All three covenant members live in intimate, self-giving relationships with one another. If people and land form a community, where the members constitute each other (make each other who they are), then it should not surprise us that serious attempts to create persistent, resilient, and resistant landscapes should foster human well-being or development.

The Hebrews saw people as having three capacities fully integrated with each other: physical, mental, and spiritual. Developing the human being implied moving on several fronts. First, it meant providing sufficient material goods to meet the basic physical needs of food, shelter, clothing, medicine, and so forth. Such development, however, also required a conscious limiting of material goods lest they become the focus of life, diverting attention from a life of service and focus from the source of all good, the Creator. Second, human development required nurturing the mind, so that people could fully utilize the creative abilities given them. Development implied growth in wisdom, reason, aesthetic and creative abilities, and practical arts. Finally, developing the human being required spiritual growth, which included not only a deep, personal relationship with the Creator, but a sense of solidarity with others and a desire to give of oneself for the good of others. Development implied placing one's life at the service of the community of

Creator and creation, of working for justice and living justly. Human development, therefore, required providing for everyone's basic physical well-being and developing the gifts of the individual within the context of strong, just community relationships. Well-developed people implied well-developed community.

While not sufficient by itself, the land-management process described above promotes physical well-being by promoting human, social, and natural capital formation. It also requires, and fosters, the building of community life, mental growth, and spiritual growth as people respond together to the requirements of managing the commons. Human development implies knowing, loving, and serving the land in communion with other people.[25] By working with the land and meeting its challenges, people grow together in wisdom and develop the ability to manage land well.

Similarly, if Creator, people, and land strongly influence one another, it should not surprise us that human development tends to create persistent, resilient, and resistant landscapes in a number of ways. First, fostering human development promotes a juster society. Juster societies bring about important changes. Human development changes people's perceptions of self-interest. As mental maps change, people come to see cooperation with other humans and ecological processes as desirable and possible. By changing mental maps and by fostering the self-giving and trust that make cooperation possible, spiritual growth greatly facilitates this process. Moreover, as more people open themselves to the Creator, the Creator can orchestrate their actions more easily to bring about a just society. The just society, in turn, reverses vicious cycles of distrust, reforms unjust institutions that bring about environmental degradation on the landscape, and facilitates community and other cooperative approaches to management. Moreover, on the largest scale changes occur that foster the well-being of creation in a way that we cannot discover due to our incapacity to escape our own humanity (the emergent principle problem at a supraglobal scale).

Second, as people grow, they come to view success and human well-being in nonmaterialistic terms. This, along with the emphasis on just relationships, leads to less resource extraction, less environmental stress, and a more equitable distribution of income. The recognition that creation and human wants have limits promotes the willingness to use safe minimum standards where appropriate.

Third, the growing emphasis on cooperating with ecological processes and "not-destroying" (the law of *bal tashhit*) encourages new understandings of problems, new types of technology, and new institutional approaches. (See discussion in chapter 3.) As people become more accepting of others and their viewpoints, society may allow more institutional and resource-management experimentation. This helps people learn what forms of self-organization work best ecologically and socially, given the characteristics of the society at that time.

Fourth, knowing that not all citizens will be ''just,'' society uses its norms and structures to encourage people to act justly even if they themselves have not become just. Similarly, it uses the standard tools of neoclassical environmental economics (taxes, subsidies, regulations) as it deems appropriate.

Fifth, recognizing that cooperative relationships with the land are important from a personal welfare and management perspective, local people increasingly will want to exert more influence as a group over land management (if they have not had it in the past). Spiritual growth limits grabs for power, transforms relationships, and reconciles people to one another. This facilitates cooperative management approaches.

Sixth, because they receive the benefits of the fruit of their land, and realize they must care for it, landowners may tend to reinvest a greater proportion of the returns from manufactured and natural capital back into their natural capital. Locals also will tend to allow far less degradation of their resources than when distant owners or managers decide on how to exploit these resources.

Finally, the increased desire of the public for ecologically rational land management and more ecologically attuned institutional structures leads to increased reform and coordination of government policies.

In short, improving land management develops people who, in turn, manage land more effectively. ''Gardening'' cultivates all of creation, stressing cooperative, self-giving relationships. It cooperates with ecological processes and recognizes the importance of seeking the help of the Master Gardener. Gardening proclaims healing and reconciliation for all of creation by the way people live.

Reflections on the Economics of the Garden

Because modern economics provides the main mental map used today to determine the way society uses resources, Bernstein concludes that economics plays the central role in any restructuring of the mental maps that guide other approaches to our environment (1981, p. 327). Let us then reflect on the differences between the economics of the Garden and the standard neoclassical economics taught today.

First, scholars of economics like to think of themselves as economists. However, the true economist in the Garden is the Creator. Classical Christian theology talks about the "economy of God," where the household is the world, the site of the Creator's activity. Economy means, in this sense, the way that the Creator interacts with, or "manages," the world (Meeks 1989). As vice-regents of the Creator, Garden economists attempt to understand how the Creator manages the world and to cooperate with that work. Neoclassical economists view the economy as a clock, the mechanisms of which can be discovered in natural laws such as the law of demand and supply. If there is a Creator, economists can ignore that fact because the Creator left the clock to run on its own.

Neoclassical economists only have to discover how the clock works to know how to control the economy. They safely can ignore interactions with the rest of creation because creation does not matter. It enters economic thought only as a source of raw materials and as a place to dump waste. Most economic theory even ignores these roles.

Garden economists realize that people live within a complex organic system that does not exhibit fixed, inevitable behaviors—they do not live in a highly predictable, clock-like machine. People depend upon the life-support functions of natural systems, systems having multiple equilibria and exhibiting dramatic shifts in state. They realize that more control over "nature" brings increasing powerlessness as natural processes become more and more disturbed and unpredictable. Garden dwellers know that, paradoxically, more power means less. Because they know the Garden, Garden economists seek to cooperate with creation as best as possible in lieu of attempting to control it. Moreover, these economists realize that forces operate at a scale beyond any human's ability to understand. Garden economists live much more humble lives as subeconomists who try to discern how the economist is managing the Garden at this point in time.

The two types of economics view scarcity differently. Neoclassical economics rests on the premise of scarce resources that must be allocated to meet the competing, insatiable wants of individuals. However, in the Garden, communities and their members restrict wants to fit within two limits: the need to maintain other-centeredness and the desire to maintain the health of the commons. Because people view themselves as part of one great Garden, they refuse to take more than they need for fear of injuring others, whether human or nonhuman, local or nonlocal. By sharing their goods with other generous people, they discover not only freedom from fear but spiritual abundance. They know that an attitude of scarcity leads one to hoard. People hoard when they fear they may run out of a good. Widespread fear causes widespread hoarding, creating the very scarcity they feared. Trusting that one will have enough leads to generosity and sharing of abundance. Persons who fall short receive. Cooperation brings good for all, private self-interest brings scarcity and inequity. Once again, more means less, and less means more.

Whereas isolated individuals inhabit the neoclassical world, people inhabit the Garden. Society consists not of a group of individuals who only buy and sell but of people who live in a multitude of relationships. The quality of those relationships in large part determines their spiritual and their physical well-being. Neoclassical economists do not have to worry about society, because, by improving individuals' consumption of goods and services, they believe they automatically improve the well-being of society as a whole. However, Garden economists have the more complicated task of providing for the needs of people and their communities. The *way* people go about satisfying human wants makes a big difference, because different ways of doing so have differing impacts on the relationships that constitute community life. The efficient production of goods and services may prove very inefficient in producing human welfare should relationships become distant and difficult to maintain.

The neoclassical individual makes rational calculations of the costs and benefits to him of a particular action, and so decides whether or not to act. People, on the other hand, do not decide that way, particularly if they live in the Garden. They live both as individuals and as part of social groupings that greatly influence who they are. Serving as head of the household of creation (on behalf of the economist), people act much as a good father or mother acts toward spouse and children. They work for the good of the family. Parents self-sacrifice for their children out of love, not out of rational calculation of the costs and benefits of their actions.[26] Generosity does not count the cost of one's actions.

The neoclassical individual also lives in a world filled only with humans. Neoclassical economics relegates creation to an objective "it" that can be manipulated with impunity. Garden economics realizes that creation is a "thou," someone of value with whom one can relate. Moreover, people rely on the ecological processes to sustain their own lives. No more than an astronaut would rip a spacecraft apart in order to amuse himself or herself on long trips would residents of the Garden destroy the ecological foundations of their spaceship earth. Knowing that the market fails due to economies of configuration, residents of the

Garden create structures that address spatial patterns while strengthening community life. Moreover, they understand that their spaceship includes not only the biophysical systems of which they are a part, but also the social systems. They tend their communities, taking care that their actions do not threaten the existence of the communities upon which they depend.[27] As such they create an ecological and social mosaic that is persistent, resilient, and resistant as time brings various disturbances to their community. They assess technological change and limit the market, creating boundaries within which the market allocates resources efficiently, thereby maintaining the social and ecological processes that sustain the economy.

Finally, whereas neoclassical economists can ignore inner attitudes and spirituality because the Creator set the economic clock in motion and left the room, Garden economists realize that motivations and relationships with the Creator matter greatly. Grasping for control brings destruction, whereas letting go of control brings life and *shalom*.

So, how do we begin? While the ideal may sound wonderful, reality falls far behind. We need our thinkers—philosophical, religious, political, social, or artistic—to help us reconsider the socioecological implications of our thought structures. We need to encounter one another—to build a public life—so that we learn to value the richness of our differences and to work together on issues of common concern. Survival in an ecologically uncertain world offers us a remarkable common ground upon which to meet and learn to cooperate. We can find some community problem of concern to many and organize neighbors to deal with it. When that problem has been dealt with, we can ask what our neighbors think next needs to be addressed. We need to spend time out-of-doors. When we travel from air-conditioned houses to air-conditioned offices in air-conditioned cars, accompanied wherever by music or educational tapes and CDs, we find it difficult to listen to creation and the Creator. If we cannot expect to find a worthy spouse (and keep him or her once found) without a lot of time and communication, no more can we expect to get to know creation without spending time and listening, particularly in silence (contemplation). We can experiment with managing our own land ecologically, learning from ancestors and neighbors. We can reexamine the potential value of the old ways and of folk wisdom. Finally, we can reexamine our lifestyles and our concepts of success. Being busy, while financially remunerative, makes it difficult to build individual, family, and community life (broadly conceived). Knowing one another takes time. Knowing one another, in turn, can challenge our model of reality and open new ways of seeing the world.[28]

We in the West would do well to return to our roots, reexamining and appropriating the insights our ancestors have to offer. By firmly rerooting ourselves and gaining nourishment thereby, and by observing the Garden and learning from it, we may flourish in our land for generations to come. Should we fail to do so, the land may expel us, as the Book of Leviticus warned.

Obviously, we have failed to master the art of gardening. However, we have hope because the Creator who made the Garden ardently wants us to learn. All we have to do is listen.

Notes

1. This DIM framework adapts Neuberger and Duffy's (1976) approach to the comparative analysis of national economic systems.

2. See Pawluk et al. (1992) for an example of the importance of traditional knowledge of soil conservation.

3. For instance, a firm whose strategy consists of high-grading timber, taking the best timber out of a stand and leaving the worst, ends up with poor quality timber stands. However, should it use the profits from high-grading to buy more land to high grade, instead of managing the land it owns, it may not care about the impact of management practices on its lands because it, in effect, makes its money by "mining" trees, not by growing them.

4. Problems dealing with lack of institutional memory, distinguishing between short- and long-term processes, beliefs that environmental problems are someone else's responsibility, and ideological commitment come from Lee (1992, pp. 76–77).

5. Boulding (1966) also notes that a great deal of historical evidence suggests that societies that lose their identities with posterity and lose their positive images of the future also lose their capacity to deal with present problems. As a result, they fall apart.

6. Human nature constrains individuals in three ways from knowing the world totally as it is. First, the human neural system screens out most of the stimuli to our sensory system to prevent our being overwhelmed by the masses of information we receive. Survival demands that we perceive a model of reality, not reality in its totality. Second, language, which is specific to a particular social group, categorizes knowledge for us and biases the way we interpret our experiences. Whereas Eskimos may recognize (and have names for) many kinds of snow and understand the characteristics of each, non-Eskimos may recognize only "snow." Therefore, the latter's experience of snow differs from the former's. Social knowledge becomes embedded in the symbol systems and implicit philosophies called language. Third, individuals interpret given experi-

ences differently and form their unique understanding of what the world is and how it operates.

7. Hess (1992) similarly argues that people's visions, their perceptions and beliefs of the way the western range should look, and the laws and policies to which these visions have given birth, have determined the landscape of the western United States. Some visions, the tolerant ones, work themselves out on the landscape via individuals' energy and their material resources, or via voluntary associations. The visions are "tolerant" because they are constrained by individuals' limited power. People with intolerant visions seek to use the power of the state to impose the landscape that certain individuals envision. Unconstrained by individual resources, these people seek Hobbesian solutions to achieving the "correct" landscape. Each vision, therefore, carries with it an understanding of the appropriate means for its implementation.

8. The problem of soil conservation does not exist when soil conservation measures themselves bring sufficient benefit to the individual to warrant implementing them. However, many proposed measures do not appear financially attractive to individuals. So, farmers fail to adopt soil-conserving measures despite their belief that they should conserve soil. From Firey's perspective, farmers will adopt these unfinancially attractive measures only if the value of conserving soil becomes embedded in social institutions. One could argue that, as a result, perceived self-interest then transcends personal financial returns to consider broader concerns of society.

9. Because of the importance of such values that glue society together and enable collective action, some authors such as Meeks (1989) argue that the market should be blocked in some spheres of society so as not to endanger social capital or social goods. Meeks points out that this requires democratic politics, which, in turn, requires communities of shared values.

Prior to writing *The Wealth of Nations* Adam Smith wrote *The Theory of Moral Sentiments*, a book that developed his moral philosophy. Smith believed that markets required moral individuals for the "Invisible Hand" to work. If people behaved as outlined in *The Theory of Moral Sentiments*, then Smith felt that individuals pursuing their own self-interest, would be guided, as if by an invisible hand, to do that which is the best for all of society. When constrained by a set of moral scruples, people would not engage in behavior that would lead to immiseration of people or monopolization of industries. Smith, however, revealed in *The Wealth of Nations* that he did not believe that people tended to act morally. Rather, he appeared pessimistic. Today, when we stress the importance of free markets and unconstrained individualism, we forget that the founder of free-market economics believed that people needed strong moral values to make the market a positive force for society.

10. This system also would empower those stakeholders normally disadvantaged and marginalized by the system.

11. The World Bank also reports that local governments often can carry out national mandates and policies more effectively than national governments, if

provided with the proper policy framework. In Japan, local authorities, polluting industries, and citizens groups negotiate openly about how to reduce pollution to meet national policy goals. Often the resulting emissions are less than required by law. The system's flexibility allows local solutions to local problems and fosters the idea of good corporate citizenship (IBRD 1992, p. 92).

12. See Ostrom (1990) for an analysis of the characteristics of CPRs that have worked over long periods of time, factors influencing the successful creation of new CPRs, and characteristics of CPRs that have failed.

13. In primogeniture, the eldest son inherits the land. This prevents the fragmentation of land as it is passed down to descendants.

14. For instance, in seven states of India, poor households obtained 14–23 percent of their income from CPRs and up to 84 percent of their livestock fodder whereas wealthy households obtained no more than 3 percent of income and 38 percent of livestock fodder (IBRD 1992, p. 142).

15. Thanks to Philip Powell for this point.

16. Thanks to Sarah Warren for this point.

17. It would be interesting to know whether or not Dryzek feels that nested CPRs inevitably exhibit administrative or bargaining modes of decision making.

18. The question is not whether someone will enforce laws and regulations, but rather how laws and regulations are formulated. The government would move away from its current central role in directing land policy. Instead it would facilitate cooperative approaches to establishing policies that the government would enforce.

19. Page numbers refer to pages of a draft of the final work.

20. Hostility may hamper cooperative approaches. Religious or secular organizations that promote reconciliation and conflict resolution may make it possible for stakeholders in such conflictive situations to work together. Indeed, churches may find such a role to be one of their most important social and environmental outreaches.

21. Where protected lands represent only a portion of the landscape requiring management, UNESCO's Man and the Biosphere program recommends conceiving of concentric circles of protection for parks: the core protected area of a park, surrounding buffers where land is managed for human use and its ecological relationship to the core area, and, finally, lands used for resource development without regard to the protected area. The latter lie, of course, farthest from the core. Many parks in the industrial and Third Worlds now work from this premise, involving local people in the surrounding area in programs that create an economic rationale for their cooperating in protecting the park and managing the buffer.

22. When markets are less than perfectly competitive (e.g., when monopolistic influences or government interfere with market forces), unfettered markets do not necessarily lead to maximum efficiency, either. For discussions of this point see any standard economics text such as Mansfield (1992) or Katz and

Rosen (1994). The market's inability to provide sufficient equity or landscape characteristics often leads societies to establish institutions, such as progressive income taxes and national park systems, to alter market results.

23. For two such approaches see Schumacher (1973, part 4) and Booth (forthcoming 1995).

24. For one attempt to examine free trade from the perspective of ecology and community see Daly and Cobb (1989).

25. This, of course, does not require everyone to be a farmer. It does require that people find ways to get in touch with creation.

26. As Paul said, "If I give away all my possessions, and if I hand over my body so that I may boast, but do not have love, I gain nothing. Love is patient; love is kind; love is not envious or boastful or arrogant or rude. It does not insist on its own way. . . . It bears all things, believes all things, hopes all things, endures all things. Love never ends." (1 Cor 13:3–8)

27. This book focuses primarily on the economics of land. For more broad-ranging, thought-provoking works that examine the implications of using community (including creation) as the focus of economic life, see Cobb (1992) and Daly and Cobb (1989).

28. Obviously, this in no way exhausts the possibilities. While the suggestions apply largely to people living in the United States (the culture I know best), readers can glean whatever is of value to them and create their own. The point is to start somewhere in some little way and allow oneself to grow.

References

Bandler, Richard, and John Grinder. 1975. *The Structure of Magic*. Palo Alto: California Science and Behavior Books.

Bennett, John W. 1975. "Ecosystem Analogies in Cultural Ecology." Pp. 273–303 in *Population, Ecology, and Social Evolution*, ed. Steven Polgar. The Hague/Paris: Mouton Publishers.

Bernstein, Brock. 1981. "Ecology and Economics: Complex Systems in Changing Environments." *Annual Review of Ecology and Systematics* 12: 309–30.

Booth, Douglas. Forthcoming, 1995. "Economic Democracy as an Environmental Measure." *Ecological Economics*.

Boulding, Kenneth E. 1966. "The Economics of the Coming Spaceship Earth." Ch. 1 in *Environmental Quality in a Growing Economy*, ed. Henry Jarrett. Baltimore: Johns Hopkins University Press.

Bromley, Daniel W. 1992. "The Commons, Property, and Common-Property Regimes." Pp. 3–15 in *Making the Commons Work: Theory, Practice, and Policy*, ed. Daniel Bromley. San Francisco: ICS Press.

Cobb, John B. 1992. *Sustainability: Economics, Ecology, and Justice*. Maryknoll, NY: Orbis.

Daly, Herman E., and John B. Cobb Jr. 1989. *For the Common Good: Redirecting the Economy Toward Community, the Environment, and a Sustainable Future*. Boston: Beacon Press.

Doppelt, Bob, Mary Scurlock, Chris Frissell, and James Karr. 1993. *Entering the Watershed: A New Approach to Save America's River Ecosystems*. Washington, D. C.: Island Press.

Dryzek, John. 1987. *Rational Ecology: Environment and Political Economy*. New York: Basil Blackwell.

Eckholm, Erik P. 1976. *Losing Ground: Environmental Stress and World Food Prospects*. New York: W. W. Norton.

Editors of *The Ecologist*, 1993. *Whose Common Future? Reclaiming the Commons*. London: Earthscan.

Erikson, Erik H. 1963. *Childhood and Society*. New York: W. W. Norton.

———. 1968. *Identity, Youth and Crisis*. New York: W. W. Norton.

Esman, Milton J., and Norman Uphoff. 1984. *Local Organizations: Intermediaries in Rural Development*. Ithaca: Cornell University Press.

Firey, Walter. 1963. "Conditions for the Realization of Values Remote in Time." Pp. 147–59 in *Sociological Theory, Values, and Sociocultural Change: Essays in Honor of Pitirim A. Sorokin*, ed. Edward A. Tiryakian. Glencoe, Illinois: Free Press.

Gottfried, Robert, David Wear, and Robert Lee. 1994. "Landscapes, Ecosystem Value, and Sustainability." Presented at the 1994 Association of Environmental and Resource Economists Workshop, "Integrating the Environment and the Economy: Sustainable Development and Economic/Ecological Modeling," June 6, at Boulder, Colo.

Hess, Karl, Jr. 1992. *Visions upon the Land*. Washington, DC: Island Press.

IBRD. 1992. *World Development Report 1992: Development and the Environment*. New York: Oxford University Press.

Innes, Judith Eleanor. 1990. *Knowledge and Public Policy: The Search for Meaningful Indicators*. New Brunswick: Transaction Publishers.

Katz, Michael L., and Harvey S. Rosen. 1994. *Microeconomics*. Burr Ridge, Ill.: Richard D. Irwin.

Lee, Robert G. 1992. "Ecologically Effective Social Organization as a Requirement for Sustaining Watershed Ecosystems." Pp. 73–90 in *Watershed Management: Balancing Sustainability and Environmental Change*, ed. Robert J. Naiman. New York: Springer-Verlag.

Long, Frederick J., and Matthew B. Arnold. 1995. *The Power of Environmental Partnerships*. New York: Dryden Press.

McKean, Margaret A. 1992. "Management of Traditional Common Lands (Iriaichi) in Japan." Pp. 63–98 in *Making the Commons Work: Theory, Practice, and Policy*, ed. Daniel Bromley. San Francisco: ICS Press.

Mansfield, Edwin. 1992. *Economics: Principles/Problems/Decisions*. New York: W. W. Norton.

Meeks, M. Douglas. 1989. *God the Economist: The Doctrine of God and Political Economy*. Minneapolis: Fortress Press.

Neuberger, Egon, and William J. Duffy. 1976. *Comparative Economic Systems: A Decision-Making Approach.* Boston: Allyn and Bacon.

Ostrom, Elinor. 1990. *Governing the Commons: The Evolution of Institutions for Collective Action.* New York: Cambridge University Press.

Pawluk, Roman R., Jonathan A. Sandor, and Joseph A. Tabor. 1992. "The Role of Indigenous Soil Knowledge in Agricultural Development." *Journal of Soil and Water Conservation* 47(4): 298–302.

Putnam, Robert D. 1993. *Making Democracy Work: Civic Traditions in Modern Italy.* Princeton: Princeton University Press.

Runge, Carlisle Ford. 1981. "Common Property Externalities: Isolation, Assurance and Resource Depletion in a Traditional Grazing Context." *American Journal of Agriculture and Economics:* 595–606.

———. 1992. "Common Property and Collective Action in Economic Development." Pp. 17–39 in *Making the Commons Work: Theory, Practice, and Policy,* ed. Daniel Bromley. San Francisco: ICS Press.

Schumacher, Ernst F. 1973. *Small Is Beautiful: Economics as if People Mattered.* New York: Harper & Row.

Tversky, Amos, and Daniel Kahneman. 1981. "The Framing of Decisions and the Psychology of Choice." *Science* 211 (January): 453–58.

Further Reading

Chapter 2

Ecosystem stability

Dover, Michael, and Lee M. Talbot. 1987. *To Feed the Earth: Agro-Ecology for Sustainable Development*. Washington, DC: World Resources Institute.

Holling, C. S. 1978. "The Nature and Behavior of Ecological Systems." Pp. 25–37 in C. S. Holling. *Adaptive Environmental Assessment and Management*. New York: John Wiley and Sons.

The Gaia hypothesis

Lovelock, James E. 1982. *Gaia: A New Look at Life on Earth*. New York: Oxford University Press.

Schneider, Stephen H. 1990. "Debating Gaia." *Environment* 32(4): 5–9, 29–32.

Introduction to Ecology (nontechnical)

Odum, Eugene. 1989. *Ecology and Our Endangered Life-Support Systems*. Stamford, Conn.: Sinauer.

Landscape ecology

Forman, Richard T., and Michel Godron. 1986. *Landscape Ecology*. New York: John Wiley and Sons.

Turner, M. G. 1989. "Landscape Ecology: The Effect of Pattern on Process." *Annual Review of Ecology and Systematics* 20: 171–97.

New perspectives on life

Cobb, John B., Jr., and Charles Birch. 1981. *The Liberation of Life: From the Cell to the Community*. New York: Cambridge University Press.

Kellert, Stephen R., and Edward O. Wilson, eds. 1993. *The Biophilia Hypothesis.* Washington, DC: Island Press.

The value of ecosystems

Costanza, Robert, et al. 1989. "The Valuation and Management of Wetland Ecosystems." *Ecological Economics* 1(4): 335–61.
Gottfried, Robert R. 1992. "The Value of a Watershed as a Series of Linked Multiproduct Assets." *Ecological Economics* 5: 145–61.

Chapter 3

Articles on various aspects of Christianity and ecology

Granberg-Michaelson, Wesley, ed. 1987. *Tending the Garden: Essays on the Gospel and the Earth.* Grand Rapids, Michigan: W.B. Eerdmans.

Ecology and scriptures

Austin, Richard C. 1988. *Hope for the Land: Nature in the Bible.* Atlanta: John Knox Press.
Brueggemann, Walter. 1977. *The Land.* Philadelphia: Fortress Press.
Dailey, Thomas F. 1992. "Creation and Ecology—the 'Dominion' of Biblical Anthropology." *Irish Theological Quarterly* 58(1): 1–13.
DeWitt, Calvin B., ed. 1991. *The Environment and the Christian: What Does the New Testament Say about the Environment?* Grand Rapids, Mich.: Baker Book House.
Hall, Douglas J. 1986. *Imaging God: Dominion as Stewardship.* Grand Rapids, Mich.: Eerdmans.
Zerbe, Gordon. 1992. "Ecology According to the New Testament." *Direction* 21(2): 15–26.

Reading the Bible ecologically; history of Christian theology and the environment

Santmire, H. Paul. 1985. *The Travail of Nature: The Ambiguous Ecological Promise of Christian Theology.* Philadelphia: Fortress Press.

Chapter 4

Acts/Consequences

Koch, Klaus. 1983. "Is There a Doctrine of Retribution in the OT?" Pp. 57–87 in *Theodicy in the Old Testament,* ed. James L. Crenshaw. Philadelphia: Fortress Press.

Schmid, H. H. 1973. "Creation, Righteousness, and Salvation: Creation Theology as the Broad Horizon of Biblical Theology." Pp. 102–17 in *Creation in the Old Testament,* ed. Bernhard W. Anderson. Philadelphia: Fortress.

Covenant and binding the chaos

Murray, Robert. 1992. *The Cosmic Covenant: Biblical Themes of Justice, Peace and the Integrity of Creation.* London: Sheed & Ward.

Grasping

Brueggemann, Walter. 1977. *The Land.* Philadelphia: Fortress Press.

Recapturing a sense of beauty in creation

Austin, Richard C. 1987. *Baptized into Wilderness: A Christian Perspective on John Muir.* Atlanta: John Knox Press.
———. 1988. *Beauty of the Lord: Awakening the Senses.* Atlanta: John Knox Press.

The Sabbath and creation

Austin, Richard C. 1988. *Hope for the Land: Nature in the Bible.* Atlanta: John Knox Press, Chs. 11–14.

Wisdom

Johnston, Robert K. (1987). "Wisdom Literature and its Contribution to a Biblical Environmental Ethic." Pp. 66–82 in *Tending the Garden: Essays on the Gospel and the Earth,* ed. Wesley Granberg-Michaelson. Grand Rapids, Mich.: Eerdmans.

Chapter 5

Buffer zones and reserves

Badger, Curtis J. 1990. "Eastern Shore Gold." *The Nature Conservancy Magazine,* July/August, 7–15.

Environmental economics—externalities, public goods, open-access property, property rights, value

Goodstein, Eban S. 1995. *Economics and the Environment.* Englewood Cliffs, NJ: Prentice-Hall. Chapters 3–7, 15.

Gottfried, Robert. 1992. "The Value of a Watershed as a Series of Linked Multiproduct Assets." *Ecological Economics* 5: 145–61.

McNeely, Jeffrey. 1988. *Economics and Biological Diversity: Developing and Using Economic Incentives to Conserve Biological Resources*. Gland, Switzerland: IUCN.

Pearce, David W., and R. Kerry Turner. 1990. *Economics of Natural Resources and the Environment*. Baltimore: Johns Hopkins University Press.

Seneca, Joseph J., and Michael K. Taussig. 1984. *Environmental Economics*. Englewood Cliffs, NJ: Prentice-Hall.

Institutions and their effect on land use

Ascher, William, and Robert Healy. 1990. *Natural Resource Policymaking in Developing Countries*. Durham, N.C.: Duke University Press.

Blaikie, Piers M. 1985. *The Political Economy of Soil Erosion in Developing Countries*. New York: Longman.

Blaikie, Piers, and Harold Brookfield. 1987. *Land Degradation and Society*. New York: Methuen.

Easter, William K., John A. Dixon, and Maynard M. Hufschmidt. 1986. *Watershed Resources Management: An Integrated Framework with Studies from Asia and The Pacific*. Boulder: Westview Press.

Faeth, Paul, Robert Repetto, Kim Kroll et al. 1991. *Paying the Farm Bill: Accounting for Environmental Costs of Agricultural Commodity Programs*. Washington, D. C.: World Resources Institute.

Irreversible change and the value of waiting

Arrow, K. J., and A. C. Fisher. 1974. "Preservation, Uncertainty, and Irreversibility." *Quarterly Journal of Economics* 88(May): 312–19.

Krutilla, J. V., and A. C. Fisher. 1975. *The Economics of Natural Environments*. Baltimore: Johns Hopkins University Press for Resources for the Future.

Land economics

Hartwick, John, and Nancy Olewiler. 1986. *The Economics of Natural Resource Use*. New York: Harper & Row.

Randall, Alan, and Emery N. Castle. 1985. "Land Resources and Land Markets." Pp. 571–606 in *Handbook of Natural Resource and Energy Economics*, eds. Allen V. Kneese, and William D. Schulze. Amsterdam: Elsevier Science Publishers B. V.

Natural capital

Folke, Carl, and Tomas Kåberger, eds. 1991. *Linking the Natural Environment and the Economy: Essays from the Eco-Eco Group*. Dordrecht, Netherlands: Kluwer Academic Publishers.

Kopp, Raymond J. 1992. "The Role of Natural Assets in Economic Development." *Resources* (Winter): 7–10.

Solórzano, Raúl, Ronnie de Camino, Richard Woodward et al. 1991. *Accounts Overdue: Natural Resource Depreciation in Costa Rica.* Washington, D. C.: World Resources Institute.

Stokoe, Peter K. 1990. "Natural Capital and Sustainability." Paper presented at CEARC Workshop on Natural Capital, March 15–16, at Vancouver.

Victor, Peter A. 1991. "Indicators of Sustainable Development: Some Lessons from Capital Theory." *Ecological Economics* 4(3): 191–213.

Population growth

Kelley, Allen C. 1988. "Population Pressures, Saving, and Investment in the Third World: Some Puzzles." *Economic Development and Cultural Change* 16(April): 449–64.

Repetto, Robert. 1989. "Population, Resources, Environment: An Uncertain Future." *Population Bulletin* 42(2): 1–43.

Ridker, Ronald G. 1992. "Population Issues." *Resources* (Winter): 11–14.

Southgate, Douglas, John Sanders, and Simeon Ehui. 1990. "Resource Degradation in Africa and Latin America: Population Pressure, Policies, and Property Arrangements." *American Journal of Agricultural Economics* (December): 1259–63.

Todaro, Michael. 1994. *Economic Development in the Third World.* 5th edition. White Plains, N.Y.: Longman.

Prerequisites for sustainability

Barbier, Edward B. 1987. "The Concept of Sustainable Economic Development." Economics Program, Offprint Series No. EC1(Summer). London: International Institute for Environment and Development.

Pearce, David W., and R. Kerry Turner. 1990. *Economics of Natural Resources and the Environment.* Baltimore: Johns Hopkins University Press. Chapters 1–3.

Repetto, Robert. 1992. "Accounting for Environmental Assets." *Scientific American* (June): 94–100.

Solow, Robert. 1992. "An Almost Practical Step Toward Sustainability." An Invited Lecture on the Occasion of the Fortieth Anniversary of Resources for the Future, (October 8). Resources for the Future.

WCED. 1987. *Our Common Future.* New York: Oxford University Press.

Resources as a constraint on growth

Hartwick, John, and Nancy Olewiler. 1986. *The Economics of Natural Resource Use.* New York: Harper & Row. Chapter 6.

Pearce, David W., and R. Kerry Turner. 1990. *Economics of Natural Resources and the Environment.* Baltimore: Johns Hopkins University Press. Chapter 19.

Chapter 6

Appalachia

Caudill, Harry M. 1963. *Night Comes to the Cumberlands, a Biography of a Depressed Area.* Boston: Little, Brown.

Appalachian Land Ownership Task Force. 1983. *Who Owns Appalachia?* Lexington: University of Kentucky.

Central America

Barzetti, Valerie, and Yanina Rovinski. 1992. *Toward a Green Central America: Integrating Conservation and Development.* West Hartford, Conn.: Kumarian Press.

Brockett, Charles D. 1988. *Land, Power, and Poverty: Agrarian Transformation and Political Conflict in Central America.* Boston: Unwin Hyman.

Leonard, H. Jeffrey. 1987. *Natural Resources and Economic Development in Central America: A Regional Environmental Profile.* New Brunswick, New Jersey: Transaction Books for the International Institute for Environment and Development.

Civicness

Palmer, Parker J. 1981. *The Company of Strangers: Christians and the Renewal of America's Public Life.* New York: Crossroads.

Putnam, Robert D. 1993. *Making Democracy Work: Civic Traditions in Modern Italy.* Princeton: Princeton University Press.

New approaches to agriculture and forestry

Altieri, Miguel A. 1987. *Agroecology: The Scientific Basis of Alternative Agriculture.* Boulder, Colo: Westview Press.

Dahlberg, Kenneth A., ed. 1986. *New Directions for Agriculture and Agricultural Research: Neglected Dimensions and Emerging Alternatives.* Lanham, Md.: Rowman and Allanheld.

Edwards, Clive A., Rattan Lal, Patrick Madden, Robert H. Miller et al., eds. (1990). *Sustainable Agricultural Systems.* Ankeny, Iowa: Soil and Water Conservation Society.

Franklin, Jerry F. 1992. "Scientific Basis for New Perspectives in Forests and Streams." Pp. 25–72 in *Watershed Management. Balancing Sustainability and Environmental Change*, ed. Robert J. Naiman. New York: Springer-Verlag.

Jackson, Wes, Wendell Berry, and Bruce Coleman, eds. 1984. *Meeting the Expectations of the Land: Essays in Sustainable Agriculture and Stewardship.* Berkeley: North Point Press.

Leonard, H. Jeffrey, ed. 1989. *Environment and the Poor: Development Strategies for a Common Agenda.* U.S.-Third World Policy Perspectives, No. 11. Washington D. C.: Overseas Development Council.

Oliver, Chad D., Dean R. Berg, David R. Larsen and Kevin L. O'Hara. 1992. "Integrating Management Tools, Ecological Knowledge, and Silviculture." Pp. 361–82 in *Watershed Management: Balancing Sustainability and Environmental Change,* ed. Robert Naiman. New York: Springer-Verlag.

Political ecology and dependency theory

Gardner, Florence, Yaakov Garb and Marta Williams. 1990. "Guatemala: A Political Ecology." The Environmental Project on Central America— EPOCA. Green Paper #5. October.

Hedström, Ingemar. 1986. *Somos Parte de un Gran Equilibrio: La Crisis Ecológica en Centroamérica.* San José, Costa Rica: Departamento Ecuménico de Investigación.

―――. 1988. *Volverán las Golondrinas? La Reintegración de la Creación desde una Perspectiva Latinoamericana.* San José, Costa Rica: Departamento Ecuménico de Investigación.

Chapter 7

Common property regimes (CPRs)

Bromley, Daniel, ed. 1992. *Making the Commons Work: Theory, Practice, and Policy.* San Francisco: ICS Press.

The Editors of *The Ecologist.* 1993. *Whose Common Future? Reclaiming the Commons.* London: Earthscan.

Meyer, Christine, and Faith Moosang, eds. 1992. *Living with the Land: Communities Restoring the Earth.* Philadelphia: New Society Publishers.

Ostrom, Elinor. 1990. *Governing the Commons: The Evolution of Institutions for Collective Action.* New York: Cambridge University Press.

The commons

The Editors of *The Ecologist.* 1993. *Whose Common Future? Reclaiming the Commons.* London: Earthscan.

Community economics and the environment

Cobb, John. 1992. *Sustainability: Economics, Ecology, and Justice.* Maryknoll, N. Y.: Orbis.

Daly, Herman E., and John B. Cobb, Jr. 1989. *For the Common Good: Redirecting the Economy Toward Community, the Environment, and a Sustainable Future.* Boston: Beacon Press.

Ecological critique of organizational structures

Dryzek, John. 1987. *Rational Ecology: Environment and Political Economy.* New York: Basil Blackwell.

Environmental partnerships

Long, Frederick J., and Matthew B. Arnold. 1995. *The Power of Environmental Partnerships.* New York: Dryden Press.

New perspectives on the relationship between humans and animals

Kellert, Stephen R., and Edward O. Wilson, eds. 1993. *The Biophilia Hypothesis.* Washington, D. C.: Island Press.
Barber, Theodore X. 1993. *The Human Nature of Birds: A Scientific Discovery with Startling Implications.* New York: St. Martin's Press.

Sustainable development

Holmberg, Johan, ed. 1992. *Making Development Sustainable: Redefining Institutions, Policy, and Economics.* Washington, D. C.: Island Press.
WCED. 1987. *Our Common Future.* New York: Oxford University Press.

Theological critique of political economy

Meeks, M. Douglas. 1989. *God the Economist: The Doctrine of God and Political Economy.* Minneapolis: Fortress Press.

Index

About the Author

Robert (Robin) Gottfried lives with his family on the Cumberland Plateau of Tennessee where he teaches and chairs the Department of Economics at Sewanee, The University of the South. He has worked on projects dealing with environment and development in Appalachia, Costa Rica, Ecuador, Guatemala, and Puerto Rico. His work includes river basin planning and forest policy in Costa Rica, interactions between shrimp ponds and mangrove forests in Ecuador, land use changes in Appalachia, the value of ecosystems, and biblical environmental theology. The interactions between ecological and social systems particularly interest him. He enjoys hiking, playing old-time Appalachian and Latin American music on his porch, talking with people, and just sitting and being quiet.